Pastoral Genetics

Pastoral Genetics

| 30331

Genetics

Theology and Care at the
Beginning of Life

Ronald Cole-Turner
Brent Waters

THE PILGRIM PRESS
CLEVELAND, OHIO

The Pilgrim Press, Cleveland, Ohio 44115
© 1996 by Ronald Cole-Turner and Brent Waters

Biblical quotations are from the New Revised Standard Version of the Bible, © 1989 by
the Division of Christian Education of the National Council of the Churches of Christ,
and are used by permission

Printed in the United States of America on acid-free paper

01   00   99   98   97   96   5   4   3   2   1

Library of Congress Cataloging-in-Publication Data

Cole-Turner, Ronald, 1948–
    Pastoral genetics : theology and care at the beginning of life /
Ronald Cole-Turner, Brent Waters.
        p.   cm.
    Includes bibliographical references and index.
    ISBN 0-8298-1077-3 (alk. paper)
    1. Genetic counseling.   2. Pastoral counseling.   I. Waters,
Brent.   II. Title.
RB155.7.C65   1996
241'.66—dc20   95-50981
                                                                    CIP

To Verlyn Barker,
for his courageous vision, wise counsel,
and enduring friendship

Contents

Acknowledgments

Conversations that led to this book were possible because both of us serve on the United Church of Christ Working Group on Science, Technology, and the Church. The principal staff person for this group, Verlyn L. Barker, provided constant encouragement. We are grateful to him and to the other members of the group for their patience during our long conversations.

We are also deeply grateful for the encouragement and wise advice given to us by Richard Brown, editor at Pilgrim Press. He knows our subject well, and his suggestions were invaluable.

In addition, Brent Waters expresses his gratitude as follows:

> Significant portions of this book were written while I was on study leave from the University of Redlands. I am grateful to President James R. Appleton for granting me the time to forsake my duties as chaplain to pursue this project. I am also thankful for the generosity of Ralph Waller, principal of Manchester College, Oxford, for the warm hospitality he provided during my study leave. Sections of the manuscript reflect revised lectures delivered at the Lutheran Theological Seminary, Gettysburg, Pennsylvania. I am grateful to Professor Duane Larson for inviting me to deliver these lectures. Rob Stuart, professor of English at the University of Redlands, read early drafts of selected sections of the manuscript, and his many helpful comments and suggestions were incorporated into later drafts. Most importantly, I remain humbly indebted to my wife, Diana, and daughter, Erin. They serve as constant reminders that the love shared by a family is a divine blessing, and that being a parent is always a mysterious gift and grace.

And Ronald Cole-Turner expresses his gratitude to many as well:

Memphis Theological Seminary deserves my deep appreciation for generous support during a sabbatical leave in the spring of 1995, during which the final revisions of the manuscript were completed, and I am personally grateful to President J. David Hester and to Dean Donald K. McKim for their encouragement. I am deeply indebted to the Center for Theology and the Natural Sciences in Berkeley and to its director, Robert J. Russell, for the invitation to participate in a three-year study, from 1992 to 1995, of the theological implications of human genetics. Ted Peters, who was the principal investigator of the study, merits special thanks for encouraging my efforts to explore the significance of genetic testing for pastors and for asking me to write two articles on this theme. Our work together in Berkeley was made possible by a grant from the United States National Institutes of Health, Center for Human Genome Research, through the program on Ethical, Legal, and Social Implications, grant number HG00487-01. I owe a particular debt to Robert J. Russell, with whom I have conversed at length about many of the ideas found here and whose thinking provides the core of chapter 5. But by far the best support came from family; from my wife, Rebecca, whose work as a psychologist so deeply adds to my appreciation of the subtle complexities of human relationships, and from my daughters, Sarah and Rachel, who daily teach me the wonder of life.

Introduction

A pregnancy undergoes genetic testing. The expectant parents wait anxiously. They wonder what will they do if a problem is found. How will they know what is right? Who will help them decide? What moral convictions and theological beliefs will guide them?

Another couple delays pregnancy. A genetic condition runs in one of their families, and they believe they should not pass it on to their children. Now they hear that a prenatal test for this condition is available. If a fetus is affected, the pregnancy can be ended. Do they proceed to pregnancy and testing? Can their Christian faith guide them at all in the direction their lives will take? In the age of genetics, is procreation still a participation in the creation, and is parenting a vocation one undertakes as a follower of Jesus Christ?

These are questions of faith and life, hope and pain, Christian conviction and advanced medicine. Expectant parents will turn to pastors for advice. But when pastors turn to the theological bookshelf for help, they will find little written about the theology and the morality of prenatal genetic testing.

A few recent books recognize the importance of the questions. In *Constructing a Public Theology,* Ronald F. Thiemann begins with three vignettes, one of which deals with a prenatal diagnosis of Down's syndrome. He then identifies the point of his book, which is to find a method for helping people of faith address "some of the difficulties Christians face in living lives shaped by the gospel in today's culture."[1]

Thiemann continues:

> Many Christians, when faced with the complicated demands inher-
> ent in such cases as these, are plagued by moral paralysis and seek
> a retreat from moral decision making. . . . Although decisions re-
> garding abortion and the care of handicapped newborns are in-
> tensely personal, they are influenced by contexts that are public and
> political in nature. The line between private and public, between the
> personal and the political, can no longer be drawn with absolute
> clarity. If moral decision making has an inevitable political dimen-
> sion, then *moral and theological reflection must seek to assist
> Christians in dealing with the public aspects of their lives.*[2]

A similar challenge comes from James Gustafson. Commenting
on the theology of Jürgen Moltmann, Gustafson writes: "I invite the
reader to see how far he or she would get making a choice about an
induced abortion in light of this theology and ethics."[3]

Despite these challenges, neither Thiemann nor Gustafson offers
specific help for those facing genetic testing. Their challenge, nonetheless, arises from an urgent need of today's pastors and is therefore critical for contemporary theology. Dramatic breakthroughs in
genetics research and the rapid growth of genetic testing are fundamentally redefining human health and human procreation.

How should Christians respond to this new situation? How should
they conceive and bear children? How should they choose whether to
test the fetus and whether to end the pregnancy? And can they still see
fetal development as a mystery and childbirth as a gift of divine creativity?

These are questions of ethics *and* theology. For the Christian, the
most basic question is not "What should I do?" It is, instead, "What is
God doing?" More fully stated, in light of what we are learning about
genetics, how are we now to understand the presence and power of
God the Creator in the genetic processes of life, including human life?

As pastors we are called to help others ask, in the words of H.
Richard Niebuhr, "'What is happening?' and then "What is the fitting
response to what is happening?'"[4] To be a Christian is to try to see the
tender hand of the Creator at work in our lives, in our bodies, and in
our procreative and parental responsibilities. To be a pastor is to invite

others to look for God in this way. Together as pastor and parishioner, we look for those times and places where God's will, judgment, and forgiveness are played out.

What is happening? What is God doing? How should we respond? These are the essential questions of Christian theology and ethics. It is not our role as pastors to answer the questions or to prescribe moral solutions, as if others were dependent on us to decipher God's will for them.

This point is particularly important for male clergy, who all too frequently still respond to female parishioners as if women were inherently less able than men to make theological and moral judgments. When the concern is a difficult pregnancy, the pregnant woman is the moral decision maker. She decides who, if anyone, will be trusted to share the burden of deliberation. If we as pastors are invited to share this burden, our task is to engage in a conversation that enables a deeper, clearer understanding and response, one that is open to the possibility of God's presence, healing, and blessing.

This book is a summons to clergy to participate in what must become a sustained conversation in the life of the church. Genetic science and technologies will transform human life. Church leaders must decide whether to guide the church in thinking theologically and critically about genetics and reproduction or whether, by default, to let the church slide further into the intellectual backwaters of contemporary life, where it will fail to serve even the faithful, much less its cultured despisers.

With unapologetic urgency we invite our colleagues in ministry to join this theological conversation. The topic is genetics: What do we know about the genetic basis of human illness, behavior, traits, and personality? And how should we use this knowledge to repair our health and modify our offspring? But our focus must be theological and pastoral. Our job is to ask about the relationship between God and genes, concentrating especially on the impact of genetic knowledge on the individual, the family, and the community.

The term "pastoral genetics" reflects our conviction that the most immediate and difficult questions genetic science and technology pose are those that are already bearing down upon the everyday lives of ordinary people. The theological and moral trauma of genetics will be understood firsthand by those who face choices forced upon them by knowledge they really wish they did not have, knowledge of those processes once left to God but now within the ability of humans to know and direct.

Genetic screening and testing will soon become widespread. Virtually everyone who has access to a reasonable level of health care will someday have to ask, "Should I participate in some sort of genetic screening?" This is occurring because genes associated with very common diseases, such as various types of cancer and Alzheimer's disease, are being identified, and there may be some medical benefit in knowing if one is especially at risk. In the not-too-distant future, many adults will likely undergo some sort of screening or test, and many more will have to consider whether they want to do so.

Not everyone, of course, has access to health care, often because of a lack of health insurance, but increasingly because advanced care (like genetic testing) is only available in major urban centers. This lack of access is a disturbing social justice concern that has been frequently addressed by the church and by political leaders. It is not yet clear how health insurance coverage will apply to genetic testing. Political and economic pressures will no doubt weigh heavily alongside concern for health. Many people do not want their insurance company knowing their genetic information, for fear this information may be used to limit coverage. Conversely, insurance companies may want to limit their costs by urging widespread testing.

Fetuses are already being tested for many genetic conditions. As research advances, more fetuses will be tested. Of all the religious concerns posed by contemporary genetics research, we believe that the most pressing concern is the one we address in this book— namely, the significance of genetic screening and counseling in regard to questions at the beginning of life.

This issue, which pastors are already facing, is the central focus of this book. But it is not the only question regarding genetics that pastors must consider, for pastors will be key interpreters of genetics for our culture and they need to be conversant with the broader impact of genetics on the lives of individuals, families, and communities. People will want to know, and clergy will certainly be asked many questions: "Does genetics eliminate freedom and moral responsibility?" "How should we regard those individuals who are affected by genetic disorders?" "Should we someday try to enhance the genes of our offspring?" Even more immediately, adults will want to know whether they should be tested for genes predisposing them to cancer or to neurological disorders and how they should respond when the tests indicate a problem. We desperately need clergy who are able to draw upon the combined insight of traditional Christianity and of contemporary genetics in order to guide modern human beings into an increasingly uncharted future.

Noting the explosion of genetic research and its seemingly inevitable application to reproduction, many believe that a new era of eugenics is dawning. If they are right, this new eugenics will come not because of government coercion, but precisely because governments allow individuals autonomy in reproduction, including the freedom to make eugenic choices. How can we have a future that is free, yet free of eugenics? Can free individuals learn to make wise genetic choices?

We believe that the best single hope for our society to avoid wholesale misuse of genetics and to learn the wisdom and restraint commensurate with our powers lies in clergy who are willing and capable to bring the moral and spiritual resources of religious traditions to the context of genetic decision making.

Pastoral genetics is not only urgent and, we believe, unavoidable, but is necessarily a multidisciplinary inquiry. Our discussion must be based on an accurate assessment of genetics. This means that clergy need to learn the rudiments of genetics and to know how to ask questions. In this book we include an introduction to genetics, which we think is basic for effective pastoral ministry today. Furthermore, since clergy need to work directly in contact with medical personnel, we must understand the social or institutional setting of contemporary applied human genetics. Therefore, we have included discussions of the institutional context of genetics.

The other side of the multidisciplinary balance is pastoral and theological. When we address questions regarding the beginning of life, our principal role is to be a pastor and a theologian. We are not called to be geneticists or genetic counselors. Our special role, when we are invited, is to help women or couples connect the experience of pregnancy with the grace and mercy of God.

How do we prepare for this task? As a starting point, clergy need to be familiar with various church teachings regarding genetics, and these are briefly summarized in chapter 1. But we must also learn about some recent developments in genetics and their role in prenatal care. Chapter 2 provides a brief summary.

Then we need to learn about the institutional setting in which prenatal genetic testing occurs and about the work of the genetic counselor. In chapter 3, we explore the role of the pastor in that setting.

We also need to become aware of the broader impact of reproductive technologies on the way we conceive and give birth. Is reproduction becoming a technologically managed process? Is it being dehumanized? We will consider these questions in chapter 4.

Next, we need to sensitize ourselves to the theological questions that women or couples ask when they learn that the children they have conceived have genetic abnormalities. Often these questions have to do with the goodness of God or with personal responsibility for the condition. Chapter 5 will address some of these questions. Then in chapter 6, we will consider the difficult question of suffering, particularly the pain associated with a genetically affected pregnancy. We will struggle with the meaning of healing amidst this suffering. Chapter 7 will turn to the hope of immortality and resurrection and ask how our medical decisions can be seen as fitting within this ultimate horizon of human destiny. A brief final chapter summarizes our discussion in a call to Christians to the vocation of prenatal parenting.

This book is written by a systematic theologian and a practical ethicist who, for more than a decade, have been in conversation over the growing role of science and technology in the contemporary world. Although we share most of our theological convictions, we have not always agreed on how belief is related to action. Our disagreements have kept us humble about the possibility of attaining anything like definitive answers to the questions we have dared to raise. Fortunately we serve a God who does not require of us that we agree but that we love kindness and walk humbly (Mic. 6:8).

It is our hope that all of us who are clergy will recover our role as theologians-in-community. We Christians believe, after all, that procreation is not merely a private act but is inexorably—even if inexplicably—linked with God's redemptive intentions for creation. Full pastoral care, therefore, is more than empathetic listening. It is a task of conversing about God, of struggling together to discern God's presence in pain and promise, of challenging one another to respond with faithfulness and courage to God's ways among us, and of staying with one another during the long silences when God is nowhere to be found.

1

Genes as a Pastoral Issue

The Reverend Ann Williams stared for a moment at the baptismal font. She was about to dip her hand in the water and administer the sacrament of baptism. Normally this is a joyous event, but today she is troubled. It is not only the great heartache and agony that led to this day that is causing her distress. Ann is wondering if she is baptizing the "right" baby.

The parents, John and Helen Porter, are both carriers of the common genetic disorder cystic fibrosis, or CF. With each pregnancy they face a one-in-four chance that their child will be born with CF, a chronic illness that primarily affects the lungs, pancreas, and sweat glands. The body produces a thick, sticky mucus that makes breathing and digestion difficult. Although great advances been made in its treatment, only about half of those with the illness survive into their early twenties. Children with CF require not only costly surgical and medical procedures, but also time-consuming home care involving a strict regimen of physical therapy, exercise, diet, and medication. In addition, the disease often creates emotional stress and anxiety within a family.

Despite these risks, John and Helen decided that they wanted to start a family. During her pregnancy, Helen agreed to undergo tests in order to learn whether the fetus would be affected. The test was positive, which meant they would give birth to a child with CF. During the testing

1

process, Helen and John met twice with a genetic counselor who explained the tests and told them that they had two options: either give birth and provide the necessary care or terminate the pregnancy. The counselor offered to arrange for the Porters to meet with couples who had children with CF.

At the suggestion of the genetic counselor, Helen and John asked Rev. Williams to meet with them. She listened sympathetically as they described their circumstances and the moral decisions they faced. They wondered if it was right to give birth to a baby who would experience suffering and probably premature death. They worried that they did not have the emotional and spiritual strength to be the parents of a child with CF. But they were also troubled by the prospect of an abortion. Was it right to end the development of an "imperfect" fetus? What were their duties and responsibilities as parents? There were also practical considerations: In addition to the financial burden, could they afford to take the time from their busy careers to provide the necessary care? Would they resent their child or feel guilty for "giving" this infant a terrible disease? Would it destroy their marriage and their hope for a family with other children?

At times the unfairness of the situation nearly overwhelmed them. What had they done to deserve this? Before they married, they knew that CF ran in both their families, and they understood that they might be at risk. But that was several years before a test for carriers had become available. They loved each other, they told themselves, and they really believed CF could not happen to them. Was God judging them for their carelessness?

Ann listened carefully to John and Helen, helping them to identify their feelings and to clarify what they valued in their marriage and careers. When appropriate, she raised theological themes, reminding them that there were no simple solutions and that God's love and forgiveness would be present in whatever decision they made. Ann conferred with the genetic counselor, asking questions of her own about genetics as well as raising questions she thought Helen and John were having trouble asking. For example, Ann asked the counselor whether there will ever be an effective treatment for CF. The counselor told Ann that the progress was encouraging but that she did not want to give the Porters false hope. Ann remembered studying genetics in high school biology, and she wished she could remember what she had learned.

Less than a week after receiving the test results, Helen and John decided to terminate the pregnancy, saying they thought it was "the lesser of two evils." The life-threatening and chronic nature of CF would be unfair to their child, they told Ann. In addition, they said that they doubted they had the necessary emotional and spiritual resources to cope with the heavy demands of caring for a child with CF.

The Porters seemed relieved, and Ann supported them in their decision. She met them at the hospital on the day the abortion was performed and spoke with them regularly over the next few weeks, listening especially for their feelings of grief, anger, and guilt.

After a few months had passed, John and Helen decided that they would try once more to have a "normal" or unaffected child before considering such alternatives as adoption or artificial insemination using donated sperm. Soon, Helen told Ann that she was pregnant and was about to go through the same screening procedures as before. This time the tests came back negative. John and Helen, as well as Ann, were overjoyed.

Following the baptism, Ann walked back to her chair behind the pulpit as the congregation sang a hymn. She was happy for John and Helen but was also troubled by all they had gone through to get to this day. The Porters seemed able to put the difficult experience behind them, and Ann wanted to do so as well. She hoped she would never again face a similar situation.

From Genes to Theology

No pastor wants to be in Ann's situation, but more and more of us will find ourselves there. Research in genetics is advancing rapidly. New genes associated with diseases are being discovered weekly, even daily, and often there is only a few months' delay between the scientific discovery and the availability of prenatal testing. With each genetic discovery, there is a growing likelihood for pregnant women to undergo some form of prenatal genetic testing. Soon, some believe, genetic screening may become a routine part of prenatal care, and then virtually every fetus will be tested. When that happens, every pastor will need to be prepared to be in Ann's situation.

More and more, we will find ourselves invited by women or couples to be present during the moral and theological soul-searching that is becoming a part of pregnancy today. When we find ourselves in that situation, we will have to call upon our best skills of pastoral care. In addition to the basic skills of patient and careful listening, we need to know how to interact with health care professionals, especially genetic counselors. We have to recognize the depth of grief that many will feel for a lost pregnancy, whether the pregnancy ends spontaneously or by abortion. We must understand and respect the complexity of families as systems in upheaval over the circumstances of a difficult pregnancy. We need to realize that genetic testing can be a crisis requiring parishioners to make life-changing decisions within a few days but that the consequences of the decisions will affect them for years to come.

Most important, however, we will need to be theologically prepared to provide the pastoral care needed by pregnant women or couples who undergo genetic screening and counseling. Beneath the medical questions and the psychological dynamics lie deep religious questions: Is God punishing me? Is the problem our fault? Should I end the pregnancy? Should there be a baptism, a name, and a memory?

People turn to pastors because we are bearers of a religious tradition. We are identified with a community, a way of life, a liturgy, a sacred text. They turn to us in crisis because they want to draw upon the richness of our community. They want theological companionship.

Parents come to us with a hunger to explore the connection be-tween God the Creator and the fetal life they have created. Their long-ing is all the more urgent when they have just been told that their fe-tus has a genetic problem. Does God create mistakes? Can God heal genetic flaws? Can medical technology relieve their suffering?

If as pastors we cannot help them find the connection between these life-and-death experiences on the one hand and their Christian faith on the other, then we should not be surprised when we hear that Christianity is no longer relevant to human existence in the modern world. In the Bible, God and procreation are profoundly joined, from the story of Abraham and Sarah and the conception of Isaac to the stories of the pregnancies of Elizabeth and Mary. If we cannot find that connection any longer, if these ancient stories are seen as myth and not theology, and if for us and for our parishioners the process of procreation is entirely a technical problem devoid of God's creativity and mercy, then once again science has displaced God in the minds of even the faithful.

Our trouble connecting the Creator with procreation arises largely from the compromise our theological tradition made with modern science during the Enlightenment. In the eighteenth and nineteenth centuries, Western Christian theology protected itself from scientific discoveries by surrendering its interest in the natural world to science and technology. Theology's domain shrank as theological interest in nature was abandoned. Theologians redefined theology as a descrip-tion of the consciousness of belief. The soul or spiritual conscious-ness—itself inexplicably detached from nature—was the private realm of religion, immune from attack by new scientific theories. Science, after all, discovered facts while theology expressed values. Science measured matter while theology appealed to the heart. Science and engineering were public tasks appropriate for men. Religion and child-rearing were concerns of the home and thus primarily the responsibil-ity of women. At best, religion played a role in culture and history but not in nature.

George S. Hendry makes this comment on our theological situation:

> The question for theology may be tentatively formulated in these
> terms: What is the place, meaning, and purpose of the world of na-

ture in the overall plan of God in creation and redemption? The question has been taken up by a number of theologians, and already some significant work has been done. But the enterprise is hampered by the fact that the question has been virtually ignored for the past two hundred years; nature has been dropped from the agenda of theology, which has been preoccupied with other themes, and, in consequence, has failed to develop resources to deal with it. The knowledge of nature has advanced by leaps and bounds during these two hundred years, while theology has been in the main concerned with other problems. There is thus a twofold leeway to be made up, if theology is to address itself to the problem of nature—one in the understanding of the shape of the problem, and the other in the development of theological resources for dealing with it.[1]

Fortunately, many of today's theologians are now repudiating the earlier separation between religion and nature. We are learning that one of the costs of that split is that theology has been too little concerned about the environmental impact of modern human life. Only recently have theologians begun to address the natural environment as a theological theme. One of our most pressing intellectual challenges today is to reconnect nature and spirit, not only for the sake of our daily lives but also for the future of the planet. Writers such as John Cobb, Rosemary Radford Ruether, Sallie McFague, and Jay McDaniel challenge us to recognize that our theology has an environmental impact.

We see another sign of the split between theology and nature when we look at the turmoil in today's church over sexuality and reproduction. How do we connect God the Creator with the procreative act and with all of the different ways in which human sexuality is expressed? While church councils agonize over the implications of these questions for ordination, theologians and ethicists such as James B. Nelson urge Christians to see the religious depth of our sexual alienation. When Western theology responded to the Enlightenment by surrendering interest in nature to science, it withdrew from theological interest in the human body, including human sexuality and reproduction. An important task of theology today is to reassert the affirmation made in the first chapter of the Bible, namely, that God creates us as sexual beings.

Part of the creative power of feminist theology and philosophy has been its criticism of the split in Western thought between God and nature. Theologians such as Ruether and historians of science such as Carolyn Merchant have pointed out the widespread tendency in the West to imagine God and rationality on one side of a great, metaphysical divide, with matter and emotion on the other. Men most often put themselves (or at least their minds) on the side of God and reason, often seeing women as inferior, material, emotional, and irrational.

Still another group of voices criticizing the separation between God and nature is heard among those contemporary theologians interested in theology and science. Writers such as Ian Barbour, John Polkinghorne, Arthur Peacocke, and Robert Russell have tried to comprehend the relationship between God and the natural world as described by science, while Roger Shinn and James Gustafson have stressed the significance of theological ethics for our relationship with nature. These writers are especially helpful in suggesting how we might think about God the Creator working through complex, intermediary natural processes such as human reproduction and genetics.

What these movements (environmental theology, theology and sexuality, feminist theology, and theology and science) have in common is the desire to reconnect God and nature, spirit and matter, soul and body. We strongly support this effort, and we have learned a great deal from these thinkers. We hope to contribute something to these efforts by focusing attention on theological questions surrounding prenatal genetic screening and counseling. We recognize that reconnecting God and the body is not simply an academic puzzle; it is quite literally vital, both for human beings and for the human place in nature. Human DNA is now becoming nature's most malleable locus. The tiny alterations we make in human genes will express themselves first in our offspring but ultimately in the impact of our offspring on the rest of nature. Our decisions about the genes of our offspring is one of the momentous questions of our age, deserving of the sort of careful consideration we must give to the question of our responsibility for the natural environment.

We owe a great deal to all these writers, and we share the conviction that theology must wholly rethink its understanding of nature and

of the relationship between God and the creation. We believe that traditional Christianity contains rich resources for our task. Therefore,
unlike some of these writers, we will try to draw upon rather than reject traditional doctrines. For example, we will try to make sense, genetically speaking, of the incarnation; for according to the tradition of
the early church, God took on our humanity, which must mean that
Christ assumed the human genome, thus connecting the molecular
details of our humanity with divinity. We will ask what relevance, if
any, the gospel accounts of Jesus as healer have for our understanding
of the genetic basis of many diseases. We will also consider whether
God can be redemptively active, not just in our religious consciousness or in our souls, but in our bodies and in the genes of our offspring.

Many of these writers would agree that Christian theology needs
to be interested not only in *creatio ex nihilo* but also in *creatio con-
tinua,* the continuing activity of the Creator in unfolding the possibilities of the creation. We agree, but to this we add that theology must
now take up special interest in *creatio in utero,* the presence and activity of the Creator in the unfolding processes of fetal development.
We will, in other words, try to reclaim for mainstream Protestant theology the conviction that God is engaged in the minute details of prenatal development.

We say "reclaim" because for so many mainstream Protestants today, the religious right has preempted the use of a text as majestic as
Psalm 139:13–14:

> For it was you who formed my inward parts;
>   you knit me together in my mother's womb.
> I praise you, for I am fearfully and wonderfully made.
>   Wonderful are your works;
> that I know very well.
>   My frame was not hidden from you,
> when I was being made in secret,
>   intricately woven in the depths of the earth.
> Your eyes beheld my unformed substance . . .

For the religious right, this biblical text has become a manifesto for a
"pro-life" position. Declining to use the text in the same way, main-

stream Protestantism has virtually declined to interpret it at all—largely because of the hiatus between God and creation that has characterized Protestantism since the Enlightenment. We want to reclaim this text, not as a strict rule governing reproduction, but as a basis for wonder in light of the creative powers of God.

To reclaim this text—indeed to reconnect God with nature in the process of human reproduction—we must stretch our theological and scientific languages until they meet each other and we are able to speak of creation *and* procreation, God *and* genes, mysteries *and* molecules. Only then will we have a theology adequate to the ancient claim that in Jesus of Nazareth, God assumed our human form. Only then will we begin to know what faithfulness to Jesus Christ requires of us in an age of genetic technology.

Teachings of the Churches on Genetics

Christian theology has had little to say about genetics, but the churches have not been reticent to provide moral guidance. The statements of the Catholic church have been the most explicit and clear, but Protestant statements have also been helpful in providing some guidance to pastors and church members.

For example, the Central Committee of the World Council of Churches adopted a 1989 statement that "stresses the need for pastoral counseling for individuals faced with difficult reproductive choices as well as personal and family decisions resulting from genetic information concerning themselves or others."[2]

The Governing Board of the National Council of Churches in 1986 took a similar position: "Each positive diagnosis confronts the prospective parents with numerous spiritual, ethical, medical, social and financial questions. Religious communities are frequently called upon to minister to and counsel with families facing such questions. The issues raised are approached differently within the various traditions, but are generally recognized to be of significant pastoral concern."[3]

This position was echoed in 1992 by the United Methodist Church: "We call on the church to support persons who, because of the likelihood of severe genetic disorders, must make difficult decisions regarding reproduction."[4] And in 1989, the United Church of Christ passed a pronouncement on genetics that declared, "We support genetic screening of pregnancies at risk, although we believe that the religious communities bear a great responsibility to supplement genetic counseling with religious understandings of genetic heath and moral choices."[5]

As all these statements imply, the Protestant churches permit abortion for genetic reasons, recognizing that it may be an appropriate choice for individual Christians and not simply a church concession to a pluralistic culture. Pastors might be justified in reading these statements as heightening pastoral responsibility without providing the resources to meet them.

At the same time, the Roman Catholic Church has been clear that abortion is never permissible, even in light of a genetic test indicating a severe disorder. A 1987 document discusses genetics and reproductive technology in careful detail. The statement recognizes that a prenatal genetic test might be performed in order to lead to some sort of therapy, and such a process is permitted. "If prenatal diagnosis respects the life and integrity of the embryo and the human fetus and is directed toward its safeguarding or healing as an individual, then the answer is affirmative."[6] The statement encourages medical developments that allow for early diagnosis and treatment of disease, even in utero. "Such diagnosis is permissible, with the consent of the parents after they have been adequately informed, if the methods employed safeguard the life and integrity of the embryo and the mother, without subjecting them to disproportionate risks."[7]

But the statement issues an absolute condemnation of testing that is followed by abortion, stating that prenatal genetic diagnosis

> is gravely opposed to the moral law when it is done with the thought of possibly inducing an abortion depending upon the results: A diagnosis which shows the existence of a malformation or a hereditary illness must not be the equivalent of a death sentence. Thus a woman would be committing a gravely illicit act if she were to request such a diagnosis with the deliberate intention of having an abortion should the results confirm the existence of a malformation or abnormality.[8]

A far less official statement appears in a book on theology and medicine produced by an interdisciplinary team of scholars who are in the Reformed tradition. Their conclusion is strikingly different from that of the Catholic statement:

> If the fetus has a condition such as anencephaly or trisomy 18 that is seemingly inconsistent with the fetus's ever becoming a person or ever coming close to having God-imaging capacities, we would recommend an abortion. And if the fetus has a condition such as Tay-Sachs disease, which can promise only an inevitably short life that is subjectively indistinguishable from torture, we would recommend an abortion. Such recommendations are, we think, morally legitimate even if they are not free from the moral ambiguity of tragedy, but they rely, of course, on accurate diagnosis.[9]

A similar opinion was offered, at the very outset of the era of prenatal genetic testing, by United Methodist historian and theologian Albert Outler: "There is, therefore, an undeniable case for some kinds of 'therapeutic' abortions, and I would be greatly interested in the exploration of this category with a view to its possible enlargement—if such explorations could start from some higher view of fetal life than mere tissue."[10]

It is now time for the church to take up the challenge of this exploration.

2

Through the Valley of the Shadow of Life

"I'm sure glad there's a test for cystic fibrosis," Henry said to the genetic counselor as he and Maria walked into the room to learn about the test results. "I couldn't deal with the uncertainty that our parents faced."

"Well, I wish it were that clear-cut," Rose said. "Many times it is, but I'm afraid your test results are not conclusive."

"Then let's have them do it over again. You won't have to run the amnio all over too, will you?" Maria asked.

"No, no. It's not that," Rose said. "They ran all the tests right. It's just that there are many forms of the cystic fibrosis gene. We can test for most of them but we can't test for them all. Henry, we know that CF runs in your family, and we're guessing that you may be a carrier for one of the forms that we can't detect. We can test for the form that Maria is carrying, and unfortunately the prenatal test was positive, so we know the fetus is carrying Maria's CF gene. What we don't know is whether the fetus has received one from you, Henry. If so, then your child will probably have CF. If not, then he or she will be a carrier and not have the disease. Trouble is, we just can't tell."

"So all we know now is that the odds are higher than one out of four, right?" Henry asked.

"That's about it," Rose said. "Pretty high odds."

"We went through all this, and that's all you can give us—just more odds?" Maria said.

Genetics is changing the process of having a baby. What was once a mystery is now rapidly becoming a technologically managed process. Pregnancies are planned, tested, treated, and sometimes terminated for genetic reasons. The genetic revolution is, first of all, a revolution in our most basic human activity: namely, procreation.

Some think that as technology advances and as childbirth becomes more managed, pastoral care will slip into the background. Conceiving and bearing a child, it is supposed, will cease to be a religious event and become only a medical procedure. Mystery gives way to diagnosis, treatment, control. God is no longer needed, and neither is the pastor or the congregation.

Such a view, we believe, is wrong. We are convinced that as technology advances, religious faith is needed more than ever. As medical genetics becomes more powerful, competent pastoral care becomes more necessary. More than ever, women or couples will need the guidance, the companionship, the consolation, and the affirmation that are found in Christian faith and community as they conceive, test, and bear children.

Despite this need, the religious dimension of childbirth may disappear nonetheless—not because theology is truly rendered irrelevant by the advance of technology in conception and birth, but for the simple reason that pastors are unable to bridge the theological and the technological realms. Pastoral care begins, we believe, not at the baptismal font or at the moment of infant dedication, but months earlier in the sophisticated procedures of today's technologically advanced prenatal medicine. Clergy need to be ready to offer prenatal pastoral care, care of the unborn, care of the woman as the one who gives birth, and care of the couple overwhelmed by uncertainty and indecision. Clergy need to be prepared to offer the theological counterpart of today's advanced prenatal medicine.

To be prepared, pastors and others who offer pastoral care will have to be familiar with the basic processes of contemporary prenatal care and understand, at a basic or introductory level, the role of genetics in these processes. In this chapter, we will summarize some of the most important recent developments in genetics. Our goal is to provide an introductory overview of contemporary genetics and prenatal medicine so that the reader will be able to provide supportive and competent pastoral care to those undergoing prenatal genetic testing.

We do not intend to offer a complete introduction to the field of applied human genetics. In fact, one point we want to make throughout this chapter is that developments in genetics are occurring so rapidly that information on specific genetic conditions needs to be updated almost constantly. Medical personnel themselves often have to consult the latest research before they can proceed with a case. There are thousands of genetic conditions, and clergy do not need to know anything at all about the overwhelming majority of them. But they do need to know the basics of genetics so they can understand some of the problems that arise during the testing and diagnostic process.

Pastors should not try to become geneticists or genetic counselors. But pastors who understand the basic processes of genetics will feel comfortable asking for help in learning about the most recent discoveries concerning a particular genetic condition. They will know how to interpret new findings that surely will be announced in the future. Clergy who understand the basics of genetics will be able to help women or couples undergoing prenatal genetic testing to ask better questions and interpret information more carefully. These pastors will not feel alienated from a strange process or intimidated by fears of inadequacy. They will recognize the limitations and the pressures under which the genetic counselors are working, and they will see their own pastoral role as complementing rather than detracting from or competing with the therapeutic process. Most important, they will be able to focus their attention on the woman or couple, and not on their own uncertainties.

The Testing Procedure

Genetic testing is a laboratory procedure that examines a sample of genetic material in order to determine the presence or absence of a particular form of a gene that is known to be related to a genetic condition or disease. When scientists discover the form of a gene related to a disease such as cystic fibrosis, it becomes possible to test individuals to see whether they have copies of the disease-related form of the gene. If so, then a genetic prediction can be made: the individual who tests positive will very likely develop the disease.

By giving a blood sample, anyone can be tested for any of the diseases for which the disease-related form of the gene has been found. Each cell of our body contains, in effect, two sets of genes. This acts like a built-in backup system. Often, if one gene does not work right, the other one does, and we never know the difference. But if both our copies of the gene do not work right, if both are disease-related, then we lose our backup protection and we develop the symptoms of the disease. Not all genetic diseases work this way, but most do.

Sometimes, medical professionals recommend to a couple that they be tested to see if they both carry one copy (but not two) of the same disease-related form of a gene. If both are "carriers" for a disease like cystic fibrosis or sickle-cell anemia, neither of them will show any symptoms; however, they run a one-in-four risk, with every pregnancy, of conceiving an affected fetus. When couples are tested, it is usually because they are aware that a genetic disease runs in their families or because they have already had a child affected with a condition that, although perhaps difficult to diagnose, might be a genetic disease.

When a couple is tested and found to be at risk—perhaps at a one-in-four level—of producing offspring with a genetic disease, pastors may play an important role in helping them understand their risk and their options. The most standard options are to remain childless, adopt children, or conceive a child through artificial insemination with donor sperm. A less common option would be to use a donor egg. A new, highly experimental option would be for them to conceive in vitro, using her eggs and his sperm, but to have the embryos tested genetically prior to implantation.[1] Only the embryos that test negative, or clear of the disease-related form of the gene, would be implanted.

It is possible, of course, not only to test those who are born, but to test the unborn. There are currently two procedures in widespread use, and both are far more difficult than a blood test. The first procedure, known as "amniocentesis," is usually performed between the twelfth and sixteenth week of pregnancy. Using ultrasound to guide them, physicians insert a needle through the abdomen and into the uterus. A small amount of the amniotic fluid that surrounds the fetus is withdrawn through the needle. Fetal cells from the fluid are then analyzed genetically.

The second method, chorionic villus sampling (CVS), can be performed as early as the seventh week of the pregnancy. With the help of ultrasound, physicians insert a thin tube through the vagina and cervix to remove a small sample of the chorionic villi, which are hairlike strands that connect the pregnancy sac to the lining of the uterus. Fetal cells from the sample are then analyzed. CVS can be done earlier in the pregnancy and often with less discomfort to the woman than amniocentesis; however, the results are not as reliable, so a second CVS or an amniocentesis is often performed to verify the finding.

Testing, of course, is not infallible. It is, after all, a human process, subject to a number of human errors. "Specimens may be mixed up," as one writer has suggested. "Rather than repeat the tests, laboratories may report equivocal results as either positive or negative. The tests themselves are subject to error."[2] Anyone entering the testing process needs to be aware of the limits of the reliability of the process itself. It may be helpful for the woman or couple, or the pastor, to discuss the past reliability of a particular laboratory in testing for the particular condition being screened.

One of the major concerns for the woman or the couple is the risk that either CVS or amniocentesis presents to the pregnancy. Both procedures pose a risk to the fetus, and they are currently estimated to cause the loss of the pregnancy in 1 to 2 percent of cases.

Research is underway on techniques for identifying fetal cells in the blood of the pregnant woman. If this is possible, a genetic test of the fetus would pose no more risk to the pregnant woman or to the fetus than any other blood test routinely administered to the woman during the course of her pregnancy. This process might someday become a routine part of prenatal care—so routine, in fact, that the pregnant woman may not be clearly informed that genetic testing is being done. If this happens, the woman or couple will be wholly unprepared to hear the news that a genetic problem has been found. As genetic testing becomes more common, even routine, pastors can play an important role in helping women and couples understand the full scope and meaning of the testing process.

Currently, because of the risk posed by amniocentesis or CVS, testing is limited to special cases, which fall roughly into four groups. First, it is very common for pregnancies to be screened by tests such as maternal serum alpha-fetoprotein (MSAFP), which can indicate a heightened risk that the fetus is affected by any of a number of genetic problems or other congenital concerns, such as neural tube defects. If the screening indicates a possible concern, it must be followed by a genetic test in order to provide more definitive results.

Second, physicians may recommend that pregnant women over the age of thirty-five be tested because the risk of a conceiving a fetus with Down's syndrome increases significantly at this age. Down's syndrome is not strictly a genetic disease but rather a chromosomal disorder which involves not one gene but an extra copy of an entire chromosome—specifically a third copy of chromosome 21. The condition is characterized by mental retardation and heightened susceptibility to other diseases.

The third group currently recommended for testing includes women who have already given birth to a child affected with what appears to be a genetic condition. Some genetic conditions are hard to diagnose. After such a birth, a woman or couple will likely want to know the risk of conceiving another fetus with the same condition. If a genetic test is available, it will usually be recommended.

The fourth group of individuals that are currently likely to be tested are women who, because of their family history and that of their mate, have some reason to think their pregnancy is at a higher-than-normal risk for a genetic disease. Prior to the test, the estimate of the risk will depend on a number of factors, including both the frequency of the disease in the family and the type of genetic pattern that the disease usually follows. Here, as elsewhere in the testing process, a genetic counselor provides helpful information.

As of the mid-1990s, prenatal genetic testing is performed in only a minority of pregnancies. But as more and more genes are found, and especially if the testing process itself become easier to perform and poses less risk to the fetus, testing will become increasingly common. In the not-too-distant future, prenatal genetic testing may become so routine as to be performed without the woman's full awareness that her fetus is being subjected to genetic tests, as distinct from other tests that are part of routine prenatal care.

But when the question of a prenatal genetic test is posed as a distinct decision, women often find it a difficult decision. Why undergo the risk of testing if the risk of disease may only be slightly higher than usual? Why test if there is no treatment other than abortion, and the woman or couple are not willing to end the pregnancy? "Deciding for or against testing makes many women feel they will be making a terrible mistake regardless of the path chosen."[3]

Once amniocentesis or CVS has been run and a sample of the fetus' genetic material has been isolated, it can be tested for any number of genetic conditions for which a gene has been discovered. We are, of course, in a period of rapid genetic discovery. New genes are being discovered quickly, and sometimes genetic samples are subjected to multiple genetic tests, or "multiplex testing." This means that a woman might undergo testing out of concern for one condition, only to learn that another genetic test was run and that a problem has been identified.

All these recent developments are hurrying us toward the day of routine, comprehensive prenatal genetic testing. Early in the 1950s, genetic research began to probe the molecular structure of the gene itself, initiating the modern revolution in genetic technology. Nowhere has the cultural impact of this revolution been felt more intensely than in human procreation. In order to understand both the power and the limits of genetic testing, clergy need to learn about some of the highlights of genetic research during the past forty years.

Genetics after Mendel

The science of genetics dates back to the 1860s and to the important discoveries of the Austrian monk Gregor Mendel. Somewhere in our education, most of us studied biology. One unit in the course was likely devoted to genetics—especially to the work of Mendel, who discovered the basic mathematical principles or laws of genetics. He experimented with pea plants and found that certain traits, such as color or the smoothness of the pea's skin, were transmitted from generation to generation in predictable ways.

Mendel did not know anything about the existence or nature of genes, but he guessed correctly that something like genes must exist in order to carry information about traits from one generation to the next. Mendel deduced that since genes do not express themselves in every generation, their message can be overridden by another message. In this way, Mendel recognized what we call "recessive traits," which are not expressed unless two copies of the message are present. If only one copy is present in an individual (a pea plant or a human being), then the individual is a carrier but does not express the trait, or is not affected. Sickle-cell and cystic fibrosis are examples of human conditions that roughly follow the rules that Mendel discovered.

These discoveries are basic to modern genetics. The problem today, however, is that contemporary genetics has gone far beyond Mendel, often in surprising ways. Those who learned the basics of Mendelian genetics often have difficulty understanding the latest news from today's molecular genetic research. For Mendel, genes were at most a conjecture, a hypothetical message unit. He had some idea of *what* they did but no idea *how.* Contemporary genetics changes that. If Mendel guessed that booklike units of information exist inside living things, today's researchers are reading the letters on the pages of these books. In 1953, Francis Crick and James D. Watson discovered the basic structure of deoxyribonucleic acid, or DNA, which is the molecule that carries genetic information. Building on that discovery, scientists have learned a great deal about *how* DNA carries that information.

Our body, of course, is composed of billions of cells. Each one contains our DNA instructions, which are unique for every individual except identical twins. These instructions guide the cells' development and functions. DNA exists in the form of long, twisted strands, which are visible through a microscope. These strands are called "chromosomes." Human beings have twenty-three pairs of chromosomes. Each chromosome contains thousands of genes, which are best thought of as locations along the chromosomes.

Along its long, twisted strand, DNA contains an extremely long series of small chemical units. These message units are bases (in contrast to acids); and there are four of them, commonly known by their abbreviations, A, C, G, and T. Somewhere between three and five billion base pairs make up the human strands of DNA found in each cell of our bodies. These bases are arranged along the DNA strand in a precise sequence, and it is the sequence that carries the information. A gene is a location on the chromosome, in which the bases spell out a message telling the cell how to form a particular protein. Genes vary in length, but ordinarily they contain thousands of bases. It is estimated that human beings have approximately seventy thousand genes altogether.

The biochemistry is at once amazingly simple and wondrously complex. A specific sequence of three bases acts as a kind of chemical message or signal that corresponds to another molecule known as an "amino acid." Just as letters correspond to sounds from which spoken words are formed, so a sequence of three bases corresponds to an amino acid, from which proteins are formed. Proteins, from which our cells are built and maintained, are composites of amino acids. By coding for a specific amino acid, then another and another until there are hundreds or even thousands, the bases in our DNA are able to carry information or instructions that guide the construction of complex proteins. Basically, each different protein in our body has its own gene. Virtually all living things on earth are believed to use the same, simple pattern of three bases coding for a specific amino acid. Through this simple pattern, life has diversified in glorious complexity.

DNA does something extraordinary beside carry information about proteins. It is also able to copy itself. Indeed, this capacity to copy itself, or to replicate, is very close to the essential meaning of life. Without the ability to replicate, DNA would disappear as fast as it might form on a lifeless planet. Because it can replicate, it can leave multiple copies of itself behind. DNA is able to form copies because it comes in a duplex form. As Crick and Watson discovered, DNA is structured like a double helix. The double strands can separate, roughly like the two sides of a zipper. The separated strands attract floating bits of DNA, which line up opposite each base on the strand to form a copy of the original.

Most of the time, the copying occurs with amazing accuracy, but not always. One of the thousands of bases contained in a gene might miscopy. Geneticists refer to this as a "mutation." It is not clear why mutations happen, although radiation and some foods and chemicals are known to play a role. A mutation can occur when egg or sperm cells are produced, and thus can be part of an individual from conception. In this case, the mutation is present in every cell of the person's body, and the person can pass the mutation on to any offspring. Or mutations can occur later in life in a specific cell and then be passed along only to cells that are copied from it. Many cancers are thought to work in this way.

Often, copy errors pose no problem. The mutated copy may work as well as the original, or it may be overridden by the second copy of the gene that we carry, or the mutated gene may code for a protein that is not part of an essential biological process. Sometimes, however, minor errors of genetic copying have major consequences for the individual's health. If a mutation occurs in a gene that codes for a protein essential to the basic life processes, then a mutation or a miscopy as small as a single base can cause severe illness or death.

Mutations are often transmitted from one generation to the next. Depending on the kind of mutation and the location of the gene, its presence may not be expressed and the person who carries it may have no idea that it is present. Very likely all human beings carry at least some unexpressed mutations, which, if expressed, would cause serious health problems. Problems arise, however, in this way: A woman and a man decide to have children, but without knowing it, they both carry a mutated form of the same gene. Suppose they both transmit the mutated or disease-related form of the gene to the child. Quite likely the child will express the condition or the disease.

The vulnerability of genes to mutations means that sometimes a child can inherit a genetic disorder from parents who are not at risk. When the sperm or the egg is produced in the body of the parent, a change in the gene or a mutation sometimes occurs, and the child inherits the mutated form of the gene. Fortunately, most mutations are harmless, but some can cause disease even when the parents are neither affected nor carriers.

In the past decade, scientists have begun to find specific gene locations and mutated forms that are connected with specific genetic diseases, such as cystic fibrosis. These discoveries make genetic testing possible. But as more is learned, the picture grows more complex. It turns out that not just one or even a handful of mutations can give rise to cystic fibrosis, but an unknown number.[4] Suppose a father carries a mutated, disease-related form of this gene that is different from the mutation, also disease-related, that is carried by the mother. Will the child have the disease? Probably so, but much more needs to be learned about the ways in which various forms of genes might interact with one another.

Because of these complex possibilities, genetic testing cannot always predict what will happen in the development of a disease. The laboratory work may be done with complete accuracy and the result may accurately show that the fetus does have the genetic trait that leads to a particular disease—even one that follows Mendelian patterns; nevertheless, the child may not have the disease. "Thus it becomes important to distinguish between *analytic sensitivity,* the ability of a test to detect the various mutations it was designed to detect, and *clinical sensitivity,* the ability of the test to detect all patients who will get, or who have, the disease."[5] Even in such a case, there are two important limits to the power of genetics to predict the child's health in the future.

First, for some reasons that are not understood, genes are not always expressed in predictable ways. The rate at which genes are predictably expressed is referred to as the "rate of expressivity." A 100 percent rate of expressivity would mean that everyone with the appropriate form of the genes would develop the predicted disease symptoms. But this is not what actually appears to happen. Scientists can get some estimate of expressivity when they compare the presence of the disease-related form of the genes in the population with the actual number of cases of the disease. "If the positive rate of the genetic test

is much higher than the observed incidence," according to a committee from the National Academy of Science, "the expressivity of the
disease-causing genotype is low; not everyone with it goes on to man-
ifest the disease."[6] When expressivity is low, then, even when a genetic test is accurately administered, its clinical sensitivity will be
low. Not everyone who tests positive will develop the disease.

When a disease-related form of a gene is newly discovered, no one
knows its rate of expressivity. So when a genetic test is first offered, its
clinical sensitivity is unknown. Only after careful comparisons are
made with older persons (who are at least past the age of the onset of
symptoms) can expressivity be determined. Once the level of reliability is determined, ambiguity still remains—especially if reliability is
relatively low. Such a genetic test has significant predictive value and
may very well be worth performing, but it also has an inherent ambiguity, limiting its power to predict. This inherent limit of the predictive
power of genetic science must be understood and respected.

Second, the genetic test cannot predict the severity of the symptoms. A good example is the familiar chromosomal disorder, Down's
syndrome. The severity of its symptoms ranges from slight to severe.
Another example is neurofibromatosis type 1 (NF1). Individuals who
have this disease develop tumors on the face and head. The severity
can range from a condition so mild it may be undetected to one so severe that it leads to early death. NF1 is a Mendelian type of genetic
condition, now known to be caused by a gene located on chromosome
17. Nevertheless, the range of the effect of this gene, or its expressivity, varies to extremes. Still another example is cystic fibrosis, which is
"highly variable in its severity, and severity cannot be predicted by genetic testing."[7] These conditions—Down's syndrome, NF1, and cystic
fibrosis—are among the most common genetic and chromosomal disorders. "To compound the difficulties and uncertainties of such [pre-
natal] decision making, many of the genetic disorders that can now be
diagnosed are highly variable in their expressivity, yet information
about severity is rarely available through prenatal diagnosis."[8]

All of this can, of course, be terribly confusing and stressful to the
woman or couple undergoing testing. Understandably, they want
clear, unambiguous information. But technical clarity—that is, med-

ical and genetic results that have no inherent ambiguity—is not possible. By understanding this in advance, clergy can help women or couples who no doubt will find it frustrating or who will imagine that genetics has greater predictive power than the research itself would support.

Some genes are now known to contain a strange type of mutation known as a "tandem repeat." A series of three bases will be repeated again and again. For instance, the gene that leads to Huntington's, a degenerative brain disease, can contain a series of repeats. A similar process has been found in fragile X syndrome, which (after Down's syndrome) is the leading cause of mental retardation among males. Interestingly, in people who do not have these diseases, a few tandem repeats are still present, up to fifty in the case of fragile X, and up to forty in the case of Huntington's. Fragile X carriers usually have 50 to 200 such repeats, and if the number of repeats exceeds about 230, the disease is expressed. Prenatal genetic tests cannot distinguish absolutely between carriers and those who will be affected.[9]

Genes are now known to interact with one another and with their cellular environment in surprisingly complex ways. In these molecular interactions, a number of mistakes can occur. Amazingly, cells have many ways to repair themselves when things go wrong. Virtually all the processes in the cell are regulated by other processes. For instance, cell growth, which is basic to the growth of the organism, must itself be regulated; otherwise, out-of-control growth will give rise to a tumor. A mutation in the genes that govern these regulatory processes can lead to cancer. In 1994, for example, genes that play a role in colon cancer were discovered. The genes are described as "genetic proofreaders" or "housekeepers." "If these housekeepers don't function," writes Robert Service, "errors accumulate in the course of many generations of cell division—and eventually a cancerous mutation occurs."[10] An even more complex process is believed to be at work in one of the breast cancer genes, BRCA1, which heightens risk for breast and ovarian cancer. For the disease to develop, a woman first inherits one altered copy of the gene, and then a mutation occurs during her lifetime. With both copies mutated, the gene is no longer able to suppress the development of tumors.[11]

Our appreciation for this complexity only grows when we recognize, as scientists are now discovering, that many other diseases and conditions are genetic even though they do not follow Mendel's rules at all. Mendelian diseases are, in fact, rare diseases, affecting only 1 to 2 percent of the population. Other diseases such as various cancers, heart disease, and mental disorders, are now generally thought to have a genetic component, even though they are not Mendelian and do not follow the simple rules of prediction. These diseases are widespread; in fact, most people worry about their risks for these non-Mendelian genetic diseases. Although genes play a role in the development of these diseases, the role is a complex one, in which interactions between genes and the environment are more important than in Mendelian conditions. The complexity grows when we recognize that the term "environment" means not just air and water but also includes such social and psychological factors as stress or trauma. Therefore, geneticists now speak of genes as conferring a *susceptibility* to these non-Mendelian diseases rather than *causing* them. It is possible that if we know in advance that we are susceptible to diseases such as Alzheimer's, colon cancer, or Huntington's, we will be anxious, chronically depressed, or even suicidal.[12] On the other hand, if we know in advance and if some changes in lifestyle or diet could help to reduce our risk, we might be especially motivated to make these changes. At this stage, no one knows how people will typically respond to long-term genetic predictions of susceptibility.

It can be confusing when we hear that a gene for some forms of a disease, such as Alzheimer's, has been discovered. Even though we are aware that the symptoms of Alzheimer's disease strike at different ages, we tend to think of it as one disease, which when it occurs, develops for the same reasons in every patient. So if Alzheimer's disease has a genetic cause, we expect it to be the same genetic cause for all patients. However, medical research is turning up a very different picture.

For some diseases in which genes play a role—especially those in which genes confer a susceptibility that does not follow a straightforward Mendelian pattern—it appears that many genes may be involved, and so there may be many genetic pathways by which the disease can develop. In a disease such as Alzheimer's, several genes are known to play a role in the early-onset form of the disease. And in 1993, researchers located a gene believed to be involved in over one-half of the cases of late-onset Alzheimer's.[13] The fact that several different genes are involved in producing the cluster of diseases we call Alzheimer's has led some to say that we should now speak of Alzheimer's *diseases*.

Colon cancer and quite a few other very widespread diseases may follow a similar pattern. A number of genes are involved in the course of these diseases' development. They work in interaction with environmental factors and perhaps with other genes in such a way as to confer heightened susceptibility but not clear Mendelian predictability. Because these diseases are so widespread, news of discoveries of genes associated with them is certain to produce anxiety and confusion in the general public: Who should be tested? Are presymptomatic individuals, who have the genes but no symptoms, to be seen as diseased? Will these individuals lose their health insurance or their jobs? It may be that "most members of the population are potential carriers of genes predisposing to a form of cancer or heart disease".[14]

Some genes appear to affect our health in more than one way. In 1995, researchers located one mutated gene that is associated with a serious genetic condition, ataxia telangiectasia (AT), *and* with many forms of cancer, two diseases that were once considered unrelated. Individuals who carry one copy of the mutation are three to four times more likely to develop cancer than are other people. Individuals who carry two copies are thought always to develop AT, which by early childhood affects many parts of the body.[15]

Other multiple effects seem to play a more positive role, perhaps explaining why genes that contribute to poor health, regardless of the pressures of natural selection, remain in the human gene pool. The best known example is the gene related to sickle-cell anemia. If both copies are present, the disease is expressed. But for those who have only one copy of the disease-related form of the gene, their carrier status seems to give them resistance to some forms of malaria. Recently it has been suggested that carriers for cystic fibrosis may have a similar resistance to cholera.

Once again, clergy can play an important role in helping people interpret the meaning of scientific news for their own life, health, and sense of well-being. As genetic research advances, it will become possible to test for more and more predispositions to these broader categories of disease that have a genetic component. This knowledge can confer great benefits. With the proper medical advice, genetic prediction can help a person avoid foods or behaviors that increase the likelihood that a disease will develop. But many are concerned that this knowledge will also be used to exclude people from life and health insurance or employment.

Conclusion

Genetic research today is proceeding at a previously unimaginable speed. It should be clear that pastors cannot keep up with the details of even the most important developments in genetics. The field is complex, and it is expanding ever more quickly. What pastors need to recognize and respect is how the complexity of genetic science belies so much of the simplistic thinking about the subject that permeates our popular culture. Despite what many people think, a genetic test is not an infallible prediction of future health. The more we know about the relationship between genes and disease, the more we see that a host of factors are involved. Genes play an important role in defining the outcome, but so do environmental factors. In popular culture, genes are often given a mythic power to cause things to happen.

If the pace of discovery overwhelms the clergy, it also overwhelms those who turn to us for help, especially when they are undergoing genetic testing. Fortunately, there is help—both for pastors and for those undergoing the testing—in this difficult task of understanding the current state of research regarding a particular genetic condition. The most important source of help is the genetic counselor, who is primarily responsible for helping the woman or couple to understand the testing process and the information that it provides. But the genetic counselor can also help the pastor, and a working relationship between pastor and genetic counselor can be fruitful and mutually enhancing. In the next chapter, we will explore the relationship between the pastor and the genetic counselor. The point for now, however, is simply this: Clergy need to be comfortable asking for information about genetics when they are helping people through the process of genetic testing. If we fail to ask others for the help they are trained to give, we will likely fail to provide the care we are called to give.

3

The Pastor's Role

Cheryl was concerned about the chance that her pregnancy might be affected by a genetic condition in her family. She was pretty sure she wanted to undergo amniocentesis, and so she met with a genetic counselor to talk about the test process and what it might show. During the meeting, she mentioned that she was very active in her church and wanted to involve several church friends and her pastor in the decisions that lay ahead.

When Cheryl asked the genetic counselor if the pastor could be present when they met to discuss the test results, Eloise said yes, but Cheryl could tell she was apprehensive about the idea.

Cheryl looked puzzled, so Eloise explained: "It's been my experience that ministers can complicate things. What's important is that you make a decision that's right for you, not that you do what I or anyone else tells you to do."

Cheryl could only imagine the kinds of experiences that Eloise might have been referring to. From friends in other churches, she had heard about pastors who had not known at all how to offer help. Worse, she had heard of a few who made it clear "what a Christian does when faced with situations like these."

Cheryl smiled and said to Eloise, "I can see you've never worked with my pastor. You'll get along fine with her."

When a woman or couple goes through the experience of genetic testing, a genetic counselor helps them understand the testing process, the results, and the options available to them. Genetic counselors are the interpretive bridge between the medical, technical procedure and the human act of decision making that must follow. As the key interpreters of the science and of the options, they are vitally important to the entire testing process. They help women and couples to interpret the testing process in human terms.

Nevertheless, we contend that when a woman or couple wants to engage in conversation on the moral or religious interpretation of the testing, its results, or their decisions in light of the results, a genetic counselor cannot provide all the necessary help. Genetic counselors will encourage women or couples to reflect on their religious or moral tradition, but they are neither trained nor employed to help people understand religious traditions or to interpret their lives and their choices in light of those traditions. The pastor helps the woman or couple interpret the testing process in theological terms.

We believe that it is possible for the pastor's role and the genetic counselor's role to complement each other in a wholesome and positive way. Our goal in this chapter is to help pastors understand the work of genetic counselors and to define their own pastoral role in relationship with them.

The Work of the Genetic Counselor

Genetic counseling is a new profession, for which the first specialized training was offered in the early 1970s. Typically, genetic counselors are graduates of master's degree programs that specialize in human genetics, with supporting work in counseling techniques. As of the mid-1990s, there are only about one thousand master's-level genetic counselors working in the United States.

A National Academy of Science report on genetic testing defines genetic counseling this way: "Genetic counseling refers to the communication process by which individuals and their family members are given information about the nature, recurrence risk, burden, risks and benefits of tests, and meaning of test results, including reproductive options of a genetic condition, as well as counseling and support concerning the implications of such genetic information."[1]

Like most new professions, genetic counseling had antecedents; in other words someone else was doing genetic counseling before genetic counselors were trained especially to do it. Typically, the early genetic counseling, which can be traced back to the late 1940s, was done by physicians, most often pediatricians. Some physicians still offer this sort of help, especially in rural areas where more comprehensive genetic services are not available.[2] More recently, in major urban medical centers, the formal work of genetic counseling was almost entirely assigned to master's-level genetic counselors. Even more recently, however, genetic testing is occurring more often in doctors' offices, which rarely employ genetic counselors. In these settings, some women "receive group counseling with or without individual assessment and counseling, some receive written information, and some receive information over the telephone prior to testing."[3]

Because of the expanding range of settings in which prenatal genetic testing may occur, and because the standards and the practices of genetic counseling vary widely, the National Academy of Science's Committee on Assessing Genetic Risks makes this recommendation: "The committee believes that genetic counseling and education must be an integral part of genetic testing; anyone who is offering, or referring for, genetic testing must provide—or refer to—appropriate genetic counseling and education prior to testing and follow-up after testing."[4]

Depending on the particular circumstances, the genetic counselor may have contact with the woman or couple over a number of months. More often, the contact is limited to a few sessions over a period of a few weeks. During that time, the genetic counselor reviews with the couple the reasons for prenatal genetic testing, such as a genetic disease that is known to be in their families or a previous pregnancy that was thought to have been affected by a genetic condition. Once the testing has occurred, the counselor then meets with the woman or couple to interpret the results and to discuss the need for repeating the test.

The genetic counselor's primary professional concern is to explain the genetic information as clearly as possible, in order to assure as far as possible that women or couples are able to understand it fully and accurately and reach their own decisions. The women or couples, of course, are experiencing extraordinary stress, which makes it very difficult for them even to hear the information, much less to understand it. Genetic counselors are fully aware of this difficulty. They are also aware of the problem we discussed in the previous chapter, namely, the inherent ambiguities of genetic prediction. The genetic counselor's task must be to say, clearly and in everyday language, what can be said on the basis of the scientific data but not to go beyond what the science can say in an effort to provide a false sense of clarity.

Clergy can play a helpful role in this process. Depending on the woman or couple, and with the prior agreement of the genetic counselor, the pastor might offer to be present in the counseling session, especially when test results are being presented. If so, the pastor's primary role will be to listen, but this listening can have two important dimensions. First, the pastor can help the woman or couple to hear and remember the information, especially the details; and after the counseling session, the pastor can help to review what was said. Second, the pastor can ask questions to clarify key points, especially about the inherent ambiguities of the testing process and about the predicted severity of the symptoms. Because of their specialized training in the use of language, clergy can be especially sensitive to the meaning of words that are used to describe the disease or condition; therefore, they may be helpful in formulating and asking questions of clarification.

Genetic counselors are aware that most people do not think in mathematical terms. Therefore, they may not find statistical estimates of risk—which are essential to the testing results—to be particularly helpful in interpreting the results to the woman or couple. Sometimes, the counselor will translate the risk into broad categories, such as low (below 5 percent), moderate (5 to 15 percent), or high (above 15 percent).[5] Because some people misunderstand percentages to be expressing a higher risk than in fact they express, some counselors will use both categories and numbers.[6] Here again, clergy who are present in the counseling situation can heed the ability of the woman or couple to comprehend complex information in what is an inherently difficult situation.

A numerical estimate of risk, however, leaves out the one piece of information that we most want to know, and that is whether we will be the unlucky one. For example, when we hear that our risk is one in a hundred to develop a particular disease, the statistical estimate does not answer our most important question: whether we will be "the one." Genetic counselors are aware that statistics are impersonal and that translating them into personal terms is impossible. Marc Lappe refers to the personal meaning of statistics as "the subjective element." He writes:

> The subjective element of risk perception governs, in yet little explored ways, a couple's choice to start a pregnancy, elect certain diagnostic tests, and/or abort a fetus. Thus, the "true" likelihood of occurrence of a given outcome (expressed as a probability) may not be as important in certain individual's minds as some other element of that outcome, such as whether or not they can live with a given condition in their newborn child. In this sense, the *perception of* the likelihood of "good" (desired) and "bad" (undesired) outcomes can have as much to do with the impression of a given condition's severity as its likelihood of recurrence.[7]

Clergy need to be aware of this complex interplay between risk and severity. The greater the severity of a disease, the less risk of its occurrence a woman or couple might accept, even if the only alternative is abortion. Conversely, if the severity is mild, a couple might accept any risk—even 100 percent—if abortion is the only alternative.

The severity of the symptoms is thus the second important question that the woman or couple will want to have answered in the genetic counseling process. Once again, clergy cannot answer this question but can play a helpful role while the woman or couple tries to come to terms with the answer. Sometimes, a couple may recoil at hearing that anything is genetically wrong with their offspring. They may not be able to hear accurately that the symptoms are relatively mild, not life threatening, or perhaps largely treatable. Conversely, they may minimize the seriousness of the prognosis or expect a miracle cure to be developed, especially since they know that advancements in medical genetics occur rapidly. Some studies suggest that couples who have previously given birth to a child affected by a severe disorder are more likely to prevent the birth of another affected child than are those couples without the previous experience.[8]

Understanding the severity of the symptoms is perhaps the most important medical consideration facing the parents. One unprecedented difficulty parents encounter today is the real prospect of gene therapy for at least a few genetic diseases. Experiments in gene therapy began in the early 1990s, and there is reasonable hope that at least some effective treatments may be on the horizon, perhaps within a decade. If this happens, then a relatively severe, life-threatening disease like CF or sickle-cell may be substantially treatable. Women or couples will need to have an accurate assessment of the prospects for future treatment of the genetic condition that affects their fetus, since this will modulate their assessment of the condition's "severity."

Social changes also affect our assessment of the severity of some genetic or chromosomal disorders. For example, in the early 1970s, when prenatal testing first became available for Down's syndrome, many assumed that it was a severe disorder with a highly negative impact on the quality of life of the affected person and his or her family. It is now widely recognized that the severity of the symptoms of Down's syndrome, which include mental limitations as well other physiological problems, can vary widely. The physiological problems often can be treated effectively. Group-home environments provide a social setting in which a person with Down's syndrome can meet the responsibilities of everyday life. The Americans with Disabilities Act removes many barriers to employment and to other institutions, and computer devices have been developed to help many who previously would have had limited mobility or communication capabilities. These medical and social changes have combined to lower many people's estimation of the "severity" of Down's syndrome and several other conditions.

It is widely recognized that there are too few trained genetic counselors, and that those who are trained and employed are simply overwhelmed by the case load they are expected to carry. This situation will likely become more severe as more genetic tests become available.

It must also be understood that genetic counselors are employed by health care institutions. While they are hired to help the counselee, they are nevertheless employees of large medical institutions and thus are subject to institutional pressures and concerns, at least to the same extent that clergy are subject to ecclesiastical constraints and pressures. Some critics go so far as to say that the genetic counselors' institutional location makes it difficult for them to serve the interests of the counselee. Barbara Katz Rothman writes that the combination of overload and institutional commitment limits the helpfulness of the counselor:

> Genetic counselors are the people hired by institutions to get the appropriate paperwork done and forms signed. That does not make them what one referred to as "amnio salesladies," but it does place constraints on their actions, if only dramatic time constraints. I saw more counselors choose not to speak of difficult issues than to open up talk of the ramifications of the counseling. . . . Overworked counselors processed clients through.9

Kathleen Nolan largely agrees: "The volume of patients is large, there is little enough time as it is to attend to patients' physical and psychological needs, and there are frequently quite prominent gaps between the social and cultural backgrounds of prenatal health care professionals and their patients."10

The relationship between the genetic counselor and the other health professionals in the hospital is also a matter of concern. Charles L. Bosk, who writes primarily about physicians who double as genetic counselors, speaks of genetic counseling as "mopping up." "The work of genetic counseling involves a significant amount of social dirty work. . . . The genetic counselors are in the basement of the prestige hierarchy, and it is to the basement that other physicians go to find help to 'mop up' messy situations."11 Other physicians would refer or "dump" to the genetic counselor difficult cases, such as those in which an infant dies.12 Rothman, writing about female, master's-level genetic counselors, obviously in a different institutional setting, notes the opposite: "When a woman did have a problem diagnosed, physicians took over and counselors had little input into decisionmaking."13 A woman who underwent a therapeutic abortion wrote to her genetic counselor under the pseudonym "Rose Green": "[I] so appreciated your putting on your lab coat and sneaking into the abortion hospital."[14] Each of these perceptions of the genetic counselor's position in the hospital may be correct. The point for clergy is that the genetic counselor is an overworked health care professional, working in a vast, hierarchical institution and subject to its values and political pressures.

While the genetic counselor will usually not make recommendations or tell counselees what other people do in similar situations, the counselor may refer counselees to a support group made up of parents who have faced the same genetic condition. Other women or couples will be freer to give their moral perspective on their circumstances. Families who are living with an affected child can help expectant parents predict the severity of the impact of the genetic condition on the family system.

Genetic counselors along with other medical professionals, especially nurses, are becoming increasingly aware of the depths of grief that women and couples may experience through the loss of a pregnancy. When this occurs for genetic reasons—whether the loss is spontaneous or the result of an abortion—the lost pregnancy is a very much-wanted one, in which the expectant parents have already invested great energy in planning and anticipation.

Women in such situations tend to see themselves as mothers who have lost a child. Barbara Katz Rothman writes:

> The mother grieves over an abortion following prenatal diagnosis as she does the death of a child. For the mother, it *is* the death of a child, a child she has held and cared for and nurtured and loved. It is not the same as an abortion to end an unwanted pregnancy, an abortion when the woman never identified herself as a mother. . . . These "selective" abortions mean the loss of a baby, a true death.[15]

A "true death" summons a real grief. "I'm a big open wound," wrote Rose Green, speaking of her own grief. "I still have the karyotype [a copy of the genetic analysis] and the one ultrasound picture of the baby which we took (surreptitiously) from the abortion clinic. Periodically, I take them out and look at them. They are all we have left of our baby."[16]

Recently, nurses, genetic counselors, and other health care professionals have begun to encourage mothers or couples who lose their babies to permit themselves to experience the event as a time of grief. A baby born dead may be clothed in special clothing, perhaps a baptism gown; and members of the family may hold the baby, take photographs, or keep a lock of hair. Hospital personnel often encourage clergy to be present, and rites appropriate in the tradition might be used to acknowledge the value of what has been lost.

The Principle of Nondirectiveness

The most difficult question a woman or a couple undergoing prenatal genetic testing face is whether to end the pregnancy. When the prognosis is for a severe disorder and when no effective treatment exists or is likely to be developed, should the pregnancy be ended? On this most distressing question, genetic counselors are the most hesitant to offer any moral judgment. Most genetic counselors observe the principle of nondirectiveness: As a matter of principle, they refuse to advise on whether or not to choose an abortion. In order to work effectively with the genetic counselor, clergy need to understand and respect this principle.

Officially, at least, genetic counselors try to adopt a position of value neutrality in respect to the information and options they present to the counselee. Their goal is to present genetic information in clear and accurate terms, but without recommendations about choices. It has been found that virtually all genetic counselors do, in fact, avoid making recommendations to the woman or couple.[17] Physicians who offer genetic counseling, however, are thought to be more directing than are master's-level genetic counselors. Physicians, after all, are trained to be prescriptive and directive.[18]

Since the earliest days of genetic counseling in the late 1940s, counselors have generally subscribed to this principle of nondirectiveness. The principle is itself grounded in one of the most widely held principles of medical ethics: namely, patient autonomy. In strong reaction to an earlier era of paternalistic and even coercive medicine—early in the twentieth century, both in the United States and especially in Nazi Germany—medical ethics since World War II insists that competent patients be free to determine their own course of treatment. Genetic counseling conforms to this principle of autonomy through its own principle of nondirectiveness.

In addition, nondirectiveness in genetic counseling is commonly thought to derive from another source, the widespread impact of Carl Rogers's "client-centered therapy." When the early genetic counseling programs were being developed, the Rogerian approach to psychotherapy and counseling was the predominant style. According to Rogers, the counselor's task is not to direct or advise but to elicit or reflect the client's own goals. This approach to counseling was merged with training in genetics in order to produce the first genetic counseling programs.

One additional factor contributing to the principle of nondirectiveness is our broader societal debate over abortion. Once again, the coincidence of events in the early 1970s is significant. Arthur Caplan suggests, in fact, that the contemporary profession of genetic counselors came into existence at precisely the time of the *Roe v. Wade* decision, which held that there is a constitutional right to privacy that protects most abortions from state control. This right has always been both politically and morally controversial. The nascent profession of genetic counseling simply could not afford to be seen as advocating abortion, even for the most severe genetic disorders. Therefore, genetic counselors committed themselves to value neutrality, especially on abortion. "An ethic of value neutrality provided some space for clinical genetics from the abortion controversy. Genetic counselors could not be accused of favoring or promoting abortion if they adhered to a strict ethic of value neutrality."[19]

Currently, genetic counselors themselves are rethinking the philosophical and psychological assumptions that undergird the nondirectiveness principle. Nondirectiveness traditionally is explained and defended on the assumption that there is a clear distinction between facts and values. "The essence of the counselor's role is that of fact provider; the essence of the counselee's role is that of value provider."[20] But are facts and values actually so separate that they can be provided by different persons? Are facts value-free?

Karen Gervais identifies three types of concerns that are being raised about the assumption of value-free facts. She calls the first type the "science argument," since it is based on the increasingly widespread belief among scientists and philosophers of science that what we take to be scientific "facts" are not simply read from nature but are dependent upon our scientific theories.[21] Whether theories are selected on a wholly arbitrary basis or whether data play a role in theory selection is of course an important question; but regardless of the role data play in theory selection, the data or the facts are themselves theoretical interpretations rather than purely objective observations.

Secondly, Gervais refers to what she calls the "ethics argument," which points to the role of social power in the development of scientific theory. If "facts" are theory-dependent, and if theories are themselves formed in part in response to social considerations, then "facts" are really social constructs that perpetuate the interests of those in power.[22] Far from being purely objective and value-free, "facts" are thus both theory-laden and value-laden, according to this argument.

The third type of argument, according to Gervais, is what she calls the "language argument," which originates in the work of philosophers of language such as W. V. O. Quine.[23] Words used by geneticists and by genetic counselors have valuative meanings. For example, genetic "defect" is a technical term referring to an anomalous form of a gene associated with a trait or disease. But "defect" is a strongly valuative term. Genetic "disorder," similarly, carries a strongly moral—indeed theological—weight, for it implies the prior existence of a correct order against which the disorder has been introduced. Other terms, like "mutation" or "mutant," have been given pejorative meanings by their use in popular culture. The point here is that one can barely talk about genetics without using terms that carry enormous emotional, moral, and religious freight. Even if there were value-free facts, they could not be communicated in a way that is value-free, since we have no value-free language. Furthermore, the social setting itself is not value-free: the "patient" or "client" comes to be helped, to be treated, and so anything that is said to the patient will carry a prescriptive force.[24] Considerations like these led the

National Academy of Science's Committee on Assessing Genetic Risks to conclude that "genetic counseling is a highly value-laden endeavor, and it is essential that genetic counselors become aware of the values and biases they bring to their work."[25]

Because of their theological education, clergy are likely to be more sophisticated in their view of language than counselees, and even more cautious than some genetic counselors, who may still think it is possible to communicate value-free facts in value-free language. Clergy may be able to play a helpful role in the genetic counseling process by expanding the critical awareness of the counselee to the moral structure of language, concepts, and the medical setting itself.

This style of nondirectiveness can pose some frustrations for counselees, who may want the counselor to tell them what to do. Often counselees will ask, "What would you do?" or a little more subtly, "What do others in this situation usually do?" Routinely, the genetic counselor will reply this way: "The important thing is not what I would do or what others do, but that you find an approach that's right for you, that you can live with." The counselor walks a fine line between being directive and being passive. "Non-directiveness should not be mistaken for passivity. . . . Some counselors, in their eagerness to be nondirective, may shrink from being interactive with clients, from fully exploring the personal implications to them."[26]

Arthur Caplan speaks of counselees being overloaded with information by well-intentioned counselors who feel morally obligated to present the counselee all the information. This desire by the counselor "may lead counselors to simply dump information onto their clients. . . . Such an exercise often leads to frustration rather than the enhancement of [counselee] autonomy."[27]

In addition to feeling overwhelmed, the counselee may also feel isolated, cut off from the social or communal connections that sustain moral identity and provide support during times of stress or of intense moral deliberation. At just the time when she most needs her extended community, the woman undergoing prenatal genetic testing may find herself relatively alone, in an alien environment (the medical setting), with a kind stranger (the genetic counselor), who consistently declines to answer the most urgent question of all: "What should I do?"

The fact that it is the woman who is thus isolated raises a distinct concern. Has our society, which is unable to achieve anything resembling consensus on therapeutic abortion, simply refused to decide by shoving the decision onto the isolated woman, as if it were just a "woman's problem"? The responsibility of a woman to make the choices that affect her health and her future is one that should not be denied or restricted. But have we as a society turned a woman's responsibility into a woman's isolation, failing to offer moral and religious support for those women who choose to make their choices within community?

Why Clergy Are Needed

We have addressed a number of concerns about the genetic counseling process and its adequacy—especially for woman or couples who want to struggle with the moral and religious implications of their experiences and choices. We have asked: Can genetic "facts" be presented without implicit values? Are genetic counselors significantly affected by their institutional setting? Can genetic counselors be expected to offer adequate help for those who grieve? Does the counseling process isolate the woman and marginalize reproductive decisions as "women's problems"? For women and couples who want religious or theological support, can genetic counselors, even the most hardworking and conscientious ones, be expected to be solely sufficient?

We believe that the obvious answer is no, and so we are convinced that clergy have an important role to play in complementing the work of genetic counselors. In particular, where the genetic counselor is nondirective, the pastor should be forthcoming about the convictions that lie at the core of our theological traditions. Pastors should acknowledge that they approach their work with explicit beliefs and values. People seek out members of the clergy because they are bearers of a theological and moral tradition and because they represent a religious, believing community. Nondirectiveness may be appropriate to the genetic counselor, but not to the pastor. The pastor cannot fully meet the counselee's needs by being as nondirective as the genetic counselor. People come to us not for help in discovering what feels right for them, but to share with us the struggle over the meaning of what God is doing in their lives and what God requires of them.

This is not to say that the pastor should decide for the woman or couple or tell them what to believe or how to respond. To have convictions—that is, to believe something—does not require that we force others to agree with us. Rather, it requires us to be honest with ourselves and with others about the content of our beliefs and, in particular, to recognize that we are sought out because we are perceived to be persons of conviction.

Almost from the beginning of American history, churches have been voluntary associations. To participate in the church is to seek the guidance of its traditions, texts, and leaders. In its decisions on abortion, the United States Supreme Court has limited the power of states to make laws restricting access to abortion. But the Court has not sought in any way to limit a woman's right to seek the guidance of her church when she is faced with a difficult pregnancy, including one that is difficult for genetic reasons. Clergy can provide theological care, addressing especially the concerns of prenatal genetic testing, within a framework of consent that is based on the woman's choice to seek theological care.

In this respect, clergy can fully support the genetic counselor's code of nondirectiveness while at the same time insisting that they are not themselves limited by it. A vital part of the genetic counseling principle of nondirectiveness is the provision that women or couples should be encouraged to draw upon their cultural and religious traditions, and that the woman herself determines who, if anyone, will help her interpret the religious and ethic meaning of the testing and of the options that arise in light of it. If the woman, consistent with this principle of nondirectiveness, chooses to seek the theological care of her pastor, then she is freely seeking someone who will not be nondirective—someone, in other words, who has convictions. Clergy show full support for the genetic counselor's principle of nondirectiveness when they are appropriately *not* nondirective.

The 1992 Code of Ethics of the National Society of Genetic Counselors requires counselors to "respect their client's beliefs [and] cultural traditions."[28] The report of the Committee on Assessing Genetic Risks makes this recommendation: "Ethnic and cultural sensitivity is particularly important—genetic counseling should be tailored to the cultural perspective of the client, with special attention to differing cultures between client and health care professionals."[29] A less official statement, resulting from a workshop on genetic counseling, discusses this principle in more detail: Genetic counselors should "help the patient to recognize and understand the emotional, cultural, and religious factors that may influence decisionmaking [and] respect the patient's wishes concerning who should participate in the genetic counseling session."[30] One large, urban genetic counseling program reports that "the couple is encouraged to seek counsel with those whose advice they value. A list of clergy who have expressed interest in our program is shared with the couple."[31]

Clergy should be ready to offer what we call "theological companionship."[32] To offer theological companionship is to offer friendship, presence, and support.

> A faithful companion to others is one who is with them to help heal injuries to the core of the human ability to respond faithfully to the ultimate limits and potentials of being human. What the faithful companion has mostly to offer is the bread of reality and symbolic bread of the word of God that can transform even the worst terrors of reality.[33]

To offer theological companionship may mean to offer to sit through the genetic counseling session, to share the uncertainty, to draw out the questions, to be present in the loss, and to help give voice to pain. Or it may be simply to sit with others in silence before a God who seems absent.

Above all, to offer theological companionship is to grieve with those who grieve and to offer them all the resources of the worshiping community. Grief over loss of a pregnancy can be far deeper than is commonly understood. "I have been completely unprepared for the magnitude of the loss, the depth of the wound," one person has said.[34]

Barbara Katz Rothman insists that a therapeutic abortion is "a true death." She continues: "What women told me made this a particularly hard death to bear was that it was profoundly isolating. No one, the mothers reported, shared their sense of loss."[35] This is why clergy are needed.

4

Making a Baby: From Procreation to Reproduction

About a year ago, June and Larry had ended a pregnancy after undergoing prenatal testing and receiving genetic counseling. Both were deeply saddened by the event but felt that it was the only thing to do. At the time, several people told them that they could try again.

Now they have just learned that June is pregnant again. But this time they are wondering about prenatal testing. "Suppose there's another problem," June asks. "Do I get another abortion and then start over again? And how many times do we keep that up?"

Larry is worried about the impact on June's health. And he's wondering about the psychological impact on both of them. "It's up and down, up and down," he says. "Maybe it's better not to know."

They still had several weeks before the usual time for amniocentesis, and so they talked with several friends, including some from church. Some of their friends wonder why they are apprehensive about going through the testing again. A few even seemed to suggest that June and Larry have a social obligation to test the pregnancy and to end it if the test is positive.

Others, however, share their concern. "I really envy my Mom," one said. "Things didn't always turn out right back then, but at least nobody blamed you if something went wrong."

If they spoke at all about such things, our ancestors would have referred to the processes of conception and childbirth as "procreation." In procreation, God the great Creator of the universe was tenderly present in the mysteries of fetal development and the miracle of birth. Human beings were largely passive participants in a process almost entirely outside their control.

Reticence about sex is gone today, and so is the sense that procreation is a mystery through which we participate in the creative work of God. We speak of reproduction but not procreation, of planning a family, of making a baby, of designing and producing our offspring. Human conception and childbirth are increasingly subjected to technological intervention and manipulation. Our growing ability to control conception and fetal development soon may be taken for granted and become part of the normal expectation of those who are seeking to be parents.

Except for mate selection and for the act of sexual intercourse, earlier generations made few decisions about procreation. They may have hoped or prayed for a healthy baby, but they were almost entirely powerless to influence nature's course. Life was perceived as a gift because parents could do little other than accept what was given at birth. With the new genetic and reproductive technologies, however, today's parents play a much more active role in the process of fetal development. Infertility and menopause, for example, are no longer absolute barriers to giving birth. An expanding range of diseases and unwelcome traits can be identified, treated, or prevented. Parents, in short, can exert much greater influence in producing the type of child they want. Conception and fetal development are processes we manage rather than mysteries in which we participate.

But on closer inspection, the mystery has not disappeared so much as been relocated. In place of the traditional sense of religious mystery that surrounded conception and fetal development, a new aura of scientific mystery, reminiscent of medieval alchemy, surrounds the rapid advances of today's genetics. Mapping the human genome has been referred to as the "holy grail" of modern science. Television and the print media cultivate an iconography of genetics, religious in fervor and salvific in its promises. When combined with reproductive and other medical technologies, will our increasing mastery of genetics usher in a new era of improved health, or is it the beginning of a brave new world of genetic and reproductive tyranny?

Exaggerating the power of genetic science may help to persuade politicians to fund research. But exaggerating its power to predict and to treat disease will no doubt also mislead the public to trust the science more than the scientists do. The general public may come to expect a great deal from genetics; in particular, they may come to expect that the emerging fusion of genetics and prenatal medicine will offer them risk-free conception and goof-proof babies. Clergy can challenge these exaggerations and the public fears and hungers that make them gospel. Pastors can question the idolatrous nature of the hope that science and medicine will save us from all pain, all deformity, and all loss.

Genetics should be neither accepted uncritically or rejected unappreciatively, and genetic medicine is neither god nor demon. Clergy may be able to recognize the rhetoric of overstatement more quickly than others. Thus they may be able to point out the exaggerated optimism of James D. Watson (codiscoverer of the structure of the DNA molecule and former director of the human genome project) when he assures the public that the purpose of the genome project is to help those who are the products of "a bad throw of the genetic dice," to live "long, healthy, and productive lives."[1] Behind the rosy picture is a more modest but likelier core: Some suffering that results from some genetic-related illnesses and disorders can potentially be eliminated or substantially reduced. Science and medicine can be profoundly determinative forces in our lives, and genetic research is rapidly increasing the power of medicine to treat us.

When we cut through the hyperbole, we find real benefits but also real risks in genetics. In this chapter, we want to consider the risks, worries, and fears, even when expressed in provocative or overstated form. We believe there is a heuristic value to worrying aloud. The rapid development of genetic and reproductive technologies calls for skeptical caution rather than naive recklessness.

The following sections summarize some of the more common objections to genetic and reproductive technologies. Our own concerns are mixed with those of other writers across the religious and political spectrum, ranging from conservative religious thinkers to feminists. Some writers we quote fear that increased medical intervention into human reproduction will inevitably prove disastrous, that it will reduce our freedom and destroy our humanity. We do not share that belief. We see these fears as possible scenarios of a grim and dehumanized future but not as the inevitable outcome of a cautious, deliberative use of this technology.

We believe, in other words, that it is possible to use prenatal genetic technology in ways that are compatible with human dignity and with a theological awareness that our lives are to be lived out in response to God's intentions for us. If people can actually use prenatal genetic technology this way, we believe that clergy will play a major role in making it possible. The cautious, deliberative use of technology will not be brought about by more-advanced technology or better medicine, but by the ability of ordinary people to reflect deeply on the impact of technology on the meaning and quality of their humanity. For many, pastoral care will be the key that opens up this reflective process. We firmly and sincerely believe that how our society uses this technology—for good or for ill—will largely hinge on the quality of religious leadership at the congregational level. Our whole point in writing this book is to enlist clergy in helping prevent the problems we now discuss.

Genes, Health, and Blame

Defining what any of us mean by "health" can be complicated and controversial. Most often, health is defined in relation to the limits of the species, and is seen as the fullness or the excellence with which the individual expresses its vitality in relation to the potential of the species. Leon Kass defines health along these lines, as

> a state of being that reveals itself in activity as a standard of bodily excellence or fitness, relative to each species and to some extent to individuals, recognizable if not definable, and to some extent attainable. If you prefer a more simple formulation, I would say that health is the "well-working of the organism as a whole," or again,

"an activity of the living body in accordance with its specific excellences."[2]

In this definition, we see the unavoidable ambiguity of the interplay of the measurable with the unmeasurable.

Every definition of health is a cultural construct, not so much given by science as fabricated from our anxieties, expectations, standards, and judgments—all of which change over time and involve both quantitative and qualitative considerations as well as objective and subjective assessments. Health is not a part of the organism but a condition of the organism as a whole, having to do with the overall function of the organism in its context. For human beings, the context in which we function is overwhelmingly cultural and technological, having little to do with the biological environment in which we evolved and nearly everything to do with the cultural environment in which we find ourselves. For example, the body's genetically based capacity to store fat was an advantage throughout our evolutionary history but today is seen as a sign of poor health. Cultural values and expectations, more than numbers such as body temperature or serum cholesterol levels, determine what we mean by "health." Cultural values change, and so our standards for what is healthy or desirable in human beings may change in the future. In the poetry of renaissance England, fair or light skin is praised as beautiful. A generation ago, a deep tan was desirable. In the 1990s, with rising rates of skin cancer and concern about atmospheric ozone depletion, beauty is being redefined once again.

The scientific discovery of genes that are linked with particular traits will not tell us whether the traits themselves are desirable or undesirable, healthy or ill. A richer cultural context of meaning must supply this interpretation. In certain cases, scientific research can show that a particular genetic condition leads to intense suffering and early death, and then there will be no serious cultural debate about labeling such a condition a disease. But where only minor impairment or slight variation from a cultural norm exists, the discovery of a gene at the basis of the condition might lead people to consider it also a disease. Will the advance of genetic knowledge be accompanied by a rise in our expectation about the standard of what it means to be a healthy, even a "normal," human being?

Geneticist Walter E. Nance describes how, in counseling a deaf couple about the heredity of deafness, he became aware that he saw their condition as a disease to be avoided while they saw it quite differently: "I suddenly realized how insensitive I had been and how value laden the words I had used were: words like 'defect,' 'abnormality,' 'affected,' 'malformation,' or 'recurrence risk' instead of more neutral terms such as 'trait,' or 'deafness,' or 'chance' instead of risk."[3] As he began to recognize the value they attached to the culture that has developed through signing, Nance was prepared to ask, "Is it any wonder that they view their deafness as a defining cultural characteristic rather than a handicap? The couple I was counseling came to the clinic not because of any concern they had about having a deaf child but rather because of their interest in learning about the cause of their own deafness."[4] Within their culture, deafness was not a disease or a limitation.

How will genetic discoveries be understood in relationship to pre-existing cultural notions of disease and health? Some claim already to see evidence of a troubling, even sinister tendency riding on the tide of increased genetic determination and control of human health. As we exert greater control over individuals' genetic traits, our minimal expectations of what constitutes good health will change. As the floor of our expectations rises, will this create a broader category of what we classify as unhealthy individuals and a correspondingly narrower range of what we regard as normal? Will the aura of science lend a false precision to our definitions of "healthy" and "normal"? What values, in terms of physical, emotional, and intellectual health, will most deeply influence our expectations? Will an individual's value, both in terms of self-worth and social utility, be measured primarily in terms of genetic criteria?

Christopher Lasch is concerned that the use of genetic criteria for health and normalcy will result in increasingly narrower limits to what we find acceptable. While it is laudable, he believes, to try to prevent a narrow range of severe illnesses and conditions, genetic research might also contribute to "our impoverished idea of what it means to lead a good life."[5] Using genetics to define good health ignores the nobility achieved in overcoming adversity; we admire those who have played well with the "unfair" genetic hands they have been dealt. Eliminating unwanted genetic traits reflects a humane impulse, but the practical consequences of what we will come to value and despise is unknown. In the future, will individuals similar to Beethoven, Helen Keller, or John Merrick (the "Elephant Man") become objects of scorn, pity, or admiration?

We do not anticipate that the moral concerns associated with genetic health will be settled through Nazi-like eugenic laws that specify when abortions must be performed or that forbid the breeding of "unfit" individuals, at least not in the United States. But our history of slavery and of continuing racism, especially the growing fear of the young African American male as a criminal threat, needs to recognized as the social and political context in which genetic advances are being made.

Troy Duster urges us to challenge the unwarranted conclusions some draw regarding a relationship between genetics, race, and criminal behavior. In the United States in the 1990s, African Americans are incarcerated at seven times the rate of white Americans.[6] Duster is quick to point out that this ratio is a very recent development and has nothing to do with a genetic predisposition toward crime among African Americans, even though this is exactly the conclusion that some will draw. What Duster fears is that the science of genetics will lend support, in popular culture, to just such an unwarranted conclusion. "Such spurious correlations are the source of false precision. It is not much of a reach to suggest that the new technologies using DNA identification will provide part of the larger context in which the imprimatur of legitimacy may yet enshrine 'genetic thinking' about crime."[7] Duster's fears were partly realized with the 1994 publication of *The Bell Curve,* which used science in the service of ideology.

In 1993, a team of researchers reported some preliminary findings concerning a genetic basis for an extremely rare form of impulsive criminal behavior.[8] An international research team studied a large family in the Netherlands that was previously known to have a high number of males who exhibited impulsive, erratic, and criminal behavior. Research led to the discovery that all the males who showed this behavior shared a mutation in the gene for monoamine oxidase A, a previously known neurotransmitter. Males who did not have the mutation did not show the behavior. The gene for monoamine oxidase A is located on the X chromosome, which means that it is inherited according to the usual X-linked pattern—namely, that mothers are carriers but rarely express the gene themselves. The researchers found that all the women in the pedigree who were necessary carriers were in fact found to test positive, although they did not express the condition. Some feared that this is a gene for crime; the journal *Science,* which is editorially careful, reported this story under the headline, "Evidence Found for a Possible 'Aggression Gene.'"[9]

Not only is the question of a relationship between genes and crime politically explosive, but the science itself is complex nearly to the point of impossibility. We expect, however, that research will continue. As it does, clergy will be called upon more and more to help interpret the results. For example, if we learn that complex behavior such as criminality is significantly explained—even for just a few individuals—by their genes, what are we to make of their human freedom and their moral responsibility? Would we ever justify screening for criminals in advance and in detaining them before they commit a crime? Probably not, but one can readily imagine the political pressure to do so.

We believe that discoveries of relationships between genes and behavior will become more and more common.[10] Clergy will need to be prepared to take a major role in interpreting these discoveries, and the theologians should be preparing now to understand and account for these discoveries within traditional theological categories of human nature.[11] These discoveries are easily misinterpreted and quickly subjected to ideological pressures.

Others fear that even if racist conclusions or state-sponsored eugenics can be avoided, it will be impossible to guard against a rising tide of subtle but coercive pressure that will be exerted upon individuals to conform to genetic expectations.[12] This will result in greater technological control over conception and fetal development to insure that genetic "fitness," however this may come to be defined, is maximized. The benefit of genetic testing is that it will give individuals the opportunity to understand their particular genetic vulnerabilities and thus to take a stronger, better informed role in maintaining their own health. For example, those with a heightened genetic risk for a particular form of cancer could be advised to take certain precautions or to undergo frequent testing. But this beneficial knowledge can quickly become an expectation and a source of blame for all who, for whatever reason, fail to heed the advice they receive.

Our collective attitude might be to tolerate those we regard as genetically "less fit," as long as they take the appropriate precautions and do not burden our health care system with "excessive" costs. This judgment will be rooted in a classic controversy that predates genetics: To what extent is our particular level of health the result of forces beyond our control, such as airborne bacteria, and to what extent is it the result of factors over which we have some control, such as diet and exercise? Are we to be praised for our health and blamed for our illness, or are we only to be pitied when we become sick? Increasingly, we are realizing that complex conditions such as illness are the result of many processes. Some of these are clearly under our control, some are clearly not; some are partly influenced by our choices, some are under the control of others. To be sick is not merely to be a victim of a disease; neither is it merely to get what we deserve. We are responsible, up to a point, for using good judgment and heeding health advice, but we do not regard ourselves as fully responsible for the specific diseases that come to us.

For example, what, if anything, should be done to (or for) competent patients who refuse to take responsibility for their health? Should they receive the same medical care for conditions they made no effort to prevent as those who took unsuccessful precautions? What (if any) legal, economic, or moral incentives should be offered to competent individuals to assume personal responsibility for their health? Should insurance companies, for instance, pay individuals diagnosed with congenital heart problems to lower their cholesterol levels, or should they raise the rates of those who refuse?

In the past, health was a combination of luck and limited judgment. An individual was born with either a strong or weak constitution, with either immunity or susceptibility to disease or illness. Within the parameters of good or bad luck, a person exercised limited judgment concerning specific activities or practices. Personal judgment was highly restricted, however, due to ignorance regarding the relationship among genes, lifestyle, and environment. At best, a few general principles involving sanitation, diet, and exercise could be followed, but it was unknown how an individual would respond to a prescribed regimen. Consequently, one's own health was primarily a private matter, with little public accountability. Medicine stressed cure rather than prevention; illness was treated as it occurred. Medical decisions were made within the privacy of a physician-patient relationship, with little regard for public accountability other than compiling statistical data. Sick individuals were viewed more as victims than as responsible individuals suffering the consequences of their decisions. In short, the modern medicine of the recent past presupposed a separation between disease or illness, on the one hand, and personal culpability on the other.

At this point in history, we are quickly learning that our genes play a major role in determining our health. This is true, not just for the so-called genetic diseases such as cystic fibrosis, but for diseases that affect nearly everyone and that range from Alzheimer's to various cancers. What genes we inherit from our parents are, of course, wholly beyond our control. They are given to us at conception, and we cannot be blamed for them. If they predispose us toward colon cancer, we can hardly be blamed for the predisposition. But knowing that we have such a predisposition, if we are advised that we can reduce our actual risk by altering our diet and we fail to do so, are we to be blamed if we then develop a tumor?

The simple, even crude metaphor of a card game is sometimes used to speak of our genetic inheritance. At conception, nature deals each of us a hand of genetic cards that determine our predispositions to disease and limits how the game of health maintenance can be played throughout our lifetime. Contemporary genetic science and reproductive technologies are attempts to stack the deck or at least to count the cards and thus to predict the future. Unfavorable cards (genes) will be detected and we will be forewarned of their possible consequences, especially if we can alter our diet or lifestyle in order to reduce our risk. Or the birth of a child who is dealt the unfavorable gene might be prevented altogether, through therapeutic abortion.

We do not foresee coercive governmental measures enforcing compliance with preferred or prohibited conduct. Rather, economic incentives may be offered to encourage "healthy" lifestyles within targeted populations. The use of incentives will need careful legal regulation. Their point must not be to blame the individual with the genetic disadvantage but to encourage everyone to maintain health. Genetic science, as it permeates popular culture, is most likely to reinforce the tendency not to blame the sick for being sick.

But do we now blame their parents? As a result of the advance of genetic research and its applications to prenatal testing, are we merely pushing the blame back to the earlier generation? Now that it is possible for parents to know something in advance of birth about the genetic condition of their offspring, are they responsible for that condition? If we ourselves are not to be blamed because we have inherited genes that predispose us to a serious illness, are our parents to be blamed for letting us be born that way?

Parental Responsibility and Freedom

Should parents be accountable for the type of children they produce? For previous generations this was a foolish and irrelevant question. But now with a growing battery of genetic screening and reproductive technologies, this question can and will be asked.

Traditionally, prenatal care was provided behind a veil of ignorance. Pregnancies developed and came to term with little advance knowledge about the health of the infant. Even with the advent of amniocentesis and other monitoring devices, diagnostic accuracy was quite limited. If an illness, abnormality, or biological "mistake" occurred, the parents—particularly the mother—were not negligent as long as they provided adequate prenatal care, received proper rest and nutrition, and refrained from drugs, alcohol, and tobacco. Such parents were pitied, not blamed.

With advances in genetics and medicine, the situation is rapidly changing. More and more frequently, parents are given warning if a genetic or chromosomal problem is present. This warning is conveyed in a social and financial context laden with values and expectations. But few clear standards of parental responsibility have yet emerged, nor are they likely to emerge in explicit form, given our culturally assumed framework of reproductive autonomy. What this means, simply, is that parents will be overwhelmed with competing expectations but told they must decide for themselves.

Expectant women or couples will wonder what standard they should use to determine if a genetic trait warrants therapeutic intervention. They will struggle to find the appropriate balance between genetic prognosis, social pressure, and their own psychological and financial ability to provide care for a child with a genetic condition. They will wonder what laws constrain them in their choices, and they will want to know what social and economic pressures can be brought to bear upon them, for instance by employers or health insurance companies. What moral, legal, or financial sanctions, if any, should be assigned to parents who choose "badly" among their options?

Prior to the rise of modern medicine, the birth of a baby with a sickness might be seen as a sign that the parents had sinned and were being punished by the gods. In more modern settings— especially as Western society began to distinguish ever more sharply between moral and spiritual goodness, on the one hand, and physical health on the other—parents were less to be blamed and more to be pitied. Their moral challenge was how best to deal with a tragic situation beyond their control. Others sympathized with them, sometimes offering to share the burden.

But now, parents are being blamed again, not for some prior sin that led to the genetic condition in the first place, but for the last-minute sin of failing to use prenatal genetics to detect the problem and to prevent it from being expressed. Our growing knowledge of genetics is changing the moral definition of parental responsibility. For parents, the moral setting shifts from dealing with a tragic fate to making decisions that will create a destiny of their choosing.

Elizabeth Kristol observes that for "the first time in history, parents are able to customize, albeit in limited ways, the kinds of children they bring into the world."[13] She fears that this will lead to "prenatal testing [which] offers a system of quality control." The joy and anticipation of expectant parents is being displaced by the anxiety to do everything technologically possible to insure the birth of a healthy baby. Kristol equates recent developments in genetic and reproductive technologies to a revolution, arguing that like "too many revolutions, its destructive social consequences may prove both far-reaching and long-lived."[14]

As the veil of ignorance covering pregnancy is lifting, our moral perception of prenatal and parental responsibilities is also changing. Parents who give birth to a child with a genetically related illness or condition may not be viewed so much as victims, but as individuals who made poor judgments. Moral blame will be attached to parents who could have prevented the birth of a child who fails to meet "normal" or "minimal" genetic expectations.

Implicit in this blame is the sense that parents who willingly give birth to a child with a genetic condition are imposing a burden on society. Part of the burden is financial; such children do cost more to care for, and some of these costs are passed along to others in an insurance pool or to taxpayers. But another part of the burden has more to do with eugenics and the genetic quality of the human race. Abby Lippman points out some ominous consequences:

> If a child with Down's syndrome is born to a woman who has refused testing, this becomes an event for which the child's mother is responsible because she could have prevented its occurrence. The individual is made into an agent of the state. . . . Given that prevention is increasingly the goal of biomedicine, with what speed will the disabilities and variations that *can* be prevented because prenatal tests for them exist become those that *should* be prevented, with testing thereby reshaping eugenics into a private process . . . ?[15]

Such a tendency is strongly condemned by the Committee on Assessing Genetic Risks: "The goal of reducing the incidence of genetic conditions is not acceptable, since this aim is explicitly eugenic; professionals should not present any reproductive decisions as 'correct' or advantageous for a person or society."[16]

Nevertheless, as Robert Blank has observed, parents may be stigmatized for bringing into the world "unnecessary persons who would not have been born if only someone had gotten to them in time."[17]

Their failure to use medical technologies that could prevent the birth of genetically "defective" infants could inspire declining compassion and increased intolerance for both parents and their "unnecessary" children. Again, as Blank has written, "the availability of technologies for prenatal diagnosis, screening, and selection may heighten discrimination against children born with congenital or genetic disorders. In fact, it may be that acceptance of selective abortion is already reducing tolerance of those living with unwanted conditions."[18]

If parents can be held accountable for producing a baby with "undesirable" genetic traits, will they be forced rather than free in their reproductive decisions? Will insurance companies, extended families, job expectations, and general social discrimination all conspire to create an irresistible pressure on parents to avoid genetic "problems" at all cost? We do expect to see this mounting pressure to avoid genetic conditions. But, paradoxically, we also expect to see a widening space of freedom for parents to seek to create, if not a "perfect" child, then "just the right" child—the child whose gender and other characteristics (to the extent that they are genetically based) can be selected and determined in advance. Parents in the future will be confronted by the irony of increased pressure and increased autonomy.

Should parents have such an autonomous right to determine their offspring genetically? An important current legal and philosophical debate is whether the rationale for access to abortion, found in a right to privacy and reproductive autonomy, should be extended to unlimited reproductive liberty, or whether reproductive liberty can and should be limited legally. Should women or couples have an unlimited right to conceive and bear just the sort of child they want? Do they have the legal right to terminate a pregnancy if the fetus is female or if it fails in any other way to meet their expectations?

While recognizing the danger of unlimited reproductive liberty in a sexist and prejudicial society, Ruth Schwartz Cowan argues nonetheless that it would not be wise to place legal limits on reproductive liberty. "The only way, in short, to prevent a future in which mothers will be able to choose the characteristics of the fetuses they will bring to term will be to violate the norms of the scientific community, return the medical community to paternalism, and restrict women's access to abortion."[19] The fear that women will seek abortions for so-cially trivial reasons does not justify a return to paternalism. Besides, Cowan argues, the fear itself is exaggerated:

> For when left free to decide, most women decide to abort for reasons that have to do with their sense of good nurturance: for example, when they feel either that this is not a time when they can nurture a child properly or this is not the fetus that will grow into a child whom they can nurture properly. Why fear a future in which ever more children will be ever more wanted by their mothers?"[20]

John Robertson argues similarly that reproductive freedom, as it is now recognized by the United States Supreme Court, entails the right to use technology to determine the condition of the fetus. Women or couples should have unlimited freedom to "acquire that sort of child that would make one willing to bring a child into the world in the first place."[21] Arguing against Robertson, Maura A. Ryan believes there should be a limit to reproductive freedom. She agrees with Robertson "that persons ought to be protected in their right to determine when and in what manner they will reproduce, and that they should be free to shape familial life in a way meaningful for them. But such a right should not be understood as unlimited, extending as far as the acquisition of a concrete human being."[22] Fundamental to being human is each person's right to self-determination, and for parents to try to predetermine their offspring genetically by trying to conceive according to a specific design is for them to limit this fundamental right of self-determination in their future child. "At what point does a being, who has been conceived, gestated, and born according to someone's specifications, become herself or himself? . . . This view of reproduction carries . . . the sense of 'ordering' or 'purchasing' children in accordance with specific parental desires, which in the end objectively devalues the child."[23]

In the simplest terms, we can put the question this way: Can a product be a person? More precisely, can one whose genetic determinants are in part the result of analysis and technical alteration be truly free to determine his or her own existence in a way that is widely regarded as essential to the meaning of humanity?

Feminist critics of reproductive technology are also wary that the new genetic technologies will perpetuate patriarchal control of reproduction and the continued subjugation of women. Patricia Spallone, for instance, insists that feminists must reevaluate their initial enthusiasm: "After a first chorus of 'reproductive technologies give women more choice', there is the question of the meaning of these technologies."[24] Choices are neither genuine nor liberating if they are merely options contrived by patriarchal medicine:

> There can only be a limited awareness of choice in a world where women do not control our own reproduction, where medical scientists armed with technologies, impose some choices at the expense of others; where reproductive options and children are bought and sold like commodities; where many Black women and minority women in Western countries, and women in "Third World" countries, are coerced into "choosing" abortion, sterilization, and dangerous contraceptives; where reproductive and genetic technologies require the physical and social subordination of women.[25]

Furthermore, Spallone objects to genetic and reproductive technologies because they reduce women to a collection of biological parts. She argues that we "do not have to accept the man-made paradoxes and the splitting up of women into parts (eggs, embryos, wombs, placenta) which has been so ingrained as to seem natural."[26] Women should not accede to "what scientists find out for us in laboratories after they have taken our insides out."[27] Reproduction should be controlled by women, Spallone argues, and not as part of a technologically managed system.

Maria Mies argues that genetic and reproductive technologies are innately patriarchal and capitalistic, inevitably leading to the exploitation of women. She writes: "We don't need this technology. Capital needs it, men need it, and both need us and others as buyers of this technology, as otherwise there would be an end to the so-called growth."[28] Genetic and reproductive technologies are innately alienating and exploitative because technological progress is not a morally neutral process but "follows the same logic in capitalist-patriarchal and socialist-patriarchal societies," whose "model is the machine."[29] Consequently, Mies calls for an international boycott of all genetic and reproductive technologies and a moratorium on publicly funded research and development. These actions are justified because these unwanted and unnecessary technologies do "not bring us and our children any kind of qualitative or quantitative improvement in our lives . . . [and] will advance even more the exploitation and humiliation of women."[30] In addition, there are larger social and political issues at stake: Since genetic and reproductive technologies are "inimical to people, women, and nature," they open "the door wide to sexism, racism, and fascism"[31] as a prelude to more heinous eugenics policies.

In a similar way, Barbara Katz Rothman argues that women experience pregnancy as "a slow process of separation; part of us goes on to become someone else." But men view it differently: "Reality is turned on its head. Babies are 'expected' and then 'delivered,' packages from outside. Babies 'arrive,' they 'enter the world.' And most insidiously of all, we 'bond' with them—as if when the cord was cut, two became one, not one became two. Women do not feel babies arrive; we feel them leave."[32] She then notes how genetic and reproductive technology treats the fetus as a separate entity that is being produced. "The technology we have developed and continue to develop reifies a male notion of pregnancy, of the making of babies. It assumes, and thus demands of women, that our experience parallel men's, that we (like men) start from separation and come (and only with caution) to intimacy."[33]

As we saw earlier, Ruth Schwartz Cowan sees less danger in reproductive technology and argues for full access to the technology and for unlimited reproductive freedom of the sort that John Robertson supports. Freedom of choice for women means something different for Abby Lippman, who sees it not primarily as freedom to use reproductive technology but as freedom to refuse to use it:

> Choice in prenatal testing means that it can be rejected by a woman without someone questioning her motives. It means that a woman could, if she wished, continue her pregnancy after a fetal diagnosis is made because we have guaranteed her help to support a child with a disability. And it means that personal actions are completely severed from public agendas so that a decrease in uptake rates [for

genetic diagnosis] from current levels might be seen to measure the effectiveness, not the failure, of prenatal screening.[34]

At this stage in the evolution of the technology, it is simply impossible to tell whether women and their offspring have more to fear from the technology than from governments who deny their access to it. We take very seriously the warning, however, that we are in the midst of a fundamental cultural redefinition of procreation—away from the natural and the mysterious to the technological and the managed. We worry about what this will do to future human offspring, whether they will be able to live as human beings after they learn that, even in the least way, they are the result of technologically mediated choice. And we worry about how men might come to view women as mothers: To the extent that children become manufactured products, will their mothers be seen as the machinery of their production, as baby-making machines?

What does it now mean to be an individual human creature, in the image of God, free and responsible before God and the human community for one's identity, condition, and behavior? What does it mean to be a parent, in particular to be a mother? Does a theological notion of individual human personhood exclude the possibility of genetic alteration?

These are pressing concerns, especially when a legal framework of reproductive autonomy is combined with a sense of technological inevitability—that if something can be done, it will be done. Robertson presumes this sort of technological inevitability when he writes that there "is no stopping the desire for greater control of the reproductive process."[35] And since reproduction "is so value-laden an area," the best moral advice that can be offered, according to Robertson, is that there "is no better alternative than leaving procreative decisions to the individuals whose procreative desires are most directly involved."[36]

But Robertson avoids the moral problem—for Christians, at least—of how we know that our desires, especially involving procreation, are right or good. This is an especially important question for Christians because we want all our desires and decisions to reflect the intentions of God our Creator and Redeemer.

Criticizing Robertson, Ted Peters has rightly observed: "I am single-mindedly interested in one thing: loving children who are already here and children yet to be. This stance derives from a theological truth and an ethical response: God loves us unconditionally and we should love one another (1 John 4:11). Although Robertson allows for no religious ideals or deontological mandates, I do."[37] It is for the sake of such ideals and mandates that some theologians argue for limits, even outright prohibitions, concerning the use of reproductive technology.

Does a theological understanding of parenthood prohibit our use of prenatal genetics? In the remainder of this chapter, we will consider the views of theologians who come very close to answering yes to this question. Our own answer is more subtle: A theological understanding of human personhood and parenthood is consistent with a cautious and limited use of prenatal genetic technology. We will argue this position in subsequent chapters. But in the following paragraphs, we will consider the views of those who see the manipulative power of prenatal genetics as incompatible with Christian theology.

Begotten or Made?

One such theologian is Oliver O'Donovan, who believes that children should be begotten and not made. The distinction is important for O'Donovan, who believes that children should be the result of their parents' being and not their will. Ideally, parents give something of themselves to their children rather than fashioning them in an image of what they want them to become. Or as O'Donovan has written: "Our offspring are human beings, who share with us one common human nature, one common human experience and one common destiny. We do not determine what our offspring is, except by ourselves being that very thing which our offspring is to become."[38]

O'Donovan goes on to argue that reproductive technologies should not be used, because they try to cheat nature, making children commodities or artifacts. Instead, human reproduction should conform to "the natural order as the good creation of God."[39] In conforming to this natural order, we "acknowledge that there are limits to the appropriateness of our 'making.'"[40]

O'Donovan's highly critical appraisal of reproductive technologies raises the central theological and moral concerns regarding a proper human relationship with nature. Should we try to "correct" a natural reproductive process that sometimes results in ill health, pain, and suffering, or is natural procreation a divinely imposed limit that should not be transgressed? In other words, do genetic and reproductive technologies aid human flourishing, or are they instruments of pride and arrogance inevitably leading to moral decay and destruction?

More specifically, are conception, fetal development, and childbirth evolving from a "mystery" to a managed process? Are the elements of "gift," "grace," and "gratitude" being lost for the sake of quality control? Does a growing ability to manipulate the characteristics of our offspring mark a rebellion against God's providential ordering of creation? In short, are recent advances in genetics and medicine a biological Babel, or should we see them as the first tentative steps toward a new creation?

According to O'Donovan, the mystery of reproduction, in which parents receive the child they have begotten, is being transformed into a series of management decisions, through which parents obtain a baby they have made. Parents may now choose the "best" method of conception, screen a fetus for genetic traits, monitor its development, and terminate an undesirable pregnancy. Ironically, what was once a highly private act is being modified into a public process requiring assorted scientific, medical, and legal experts. Admittedly managed reproduction prevents many illnesses and disorders, thereby reducing individual suffering and improving public health. O'Donovan believes, however, that the price of displacing the mystery is too high.

In developing his arguments, O'Donovan uses the phrase, "begotten not made," which originates in the theology of the Nicene Creed. Its meaning in that context is very precisely applied to Jesus Christ, whose eternal nature as the preexistent Logos is that of one who is begotten of the very being of God, not made by God. Arius, who is rejected by the creed, had argued that Christ is a creature (i.e., made) in much the same way that all of us are. O'Donovan argues that inasmuch as the Christ is begotten and not made, this suggests a normative pattern which should be emulated in human procreation.[41] However, it is not clear that all technological intervention into human procreation disrupts the normative pattern of begetting, or whether some limited forms of intervention can be rightly used to assist in begetting our offspring. What can be inferred from the begetting of the eternal Logos to the use of technology in the procreation of children?

Furthermore, O'Donovan may also make too rigid a separation between being and will. It is again not clear to what extent the assertion of human will in procreation transgresses or interferes with divinely ordained limits. The opening chapter of Genesis contains the command to reproduce, thus placing procreation in the moral realm of responsible and intentional action. Throughout Genesis, the characters expend great effort to secure just the right mate, thereby reflecting an intentional effort to conform to God's command. Human procreation is not wholly separate from human intention and human intervention.

Despite these ambiguities in O'Donovan's argument, we find that he provides a helpful and provocative framework, particularly in his view that the resurrection of Jesus Christ is the core of Christian ethics, and we will draw more extensively on his work in later chapters.

Another helpful theologian is Stanley Hauerwas, who rightly notes the confusing ways in which biological assumptions play into our moral and legal arguments about reproduction. For example, in vitro fertilization is justified by "the assumption that biology has some extremely important role to play in parenting."[42] And another technique, surrogacy, "is defended [because it] seems to make biological parenting secondary."[43] Hauerwas fears that the state of available technology, which defines infertility or genetic traits as medical "problems," reduces children to artifacts of parental self-fulfillment rather than receiving them as "gifts necessary to sustain a people whose task is to witness to the sovereignty of God."[44] Reproductive and genetic technologies undermine or bypass the theological, moral, and natural foundations of parenthood. Technology is used to displace normal reproduction and, according to O'Donovan, remove "natural constraints" so that "more is left open to human decision."[45]

This transformation of reproduction is also reducing our capacity to endure suffering and accept tragedy. When procreation was thought to be a mystery, suffering was accepted as an unavoidable risk. Every parent faced the possible tragedy of giving birth to a seriously ill baby. Now, however, we think that suffering is never beneficial and should be prevented whenever it is within our power to do so. And so we consider ourselves justified in preventing the birth of fetuses diagnosed with debilitating illnesses or disorders because it is better to "spare them a lifetime of suffering."[46] Hauerwas asks, "in the very attempt to escape suffering, do we not lose something of our own humanity? We rightly try to avoid unnecessary suffering, but it also seems that we are never quite what we should be until we recognize the necessity and inevitability of suffering in our lives."[47] Our shrinking capacity to accept and endure suffering means that the purpose of genetic and reproductive technologies is not the improvement of health care but the "eradication of tragedy."[48]

Hauerwas's concerns about the rejection of suffering are most helpful when they refer to our own suffering and not the suffering of others. In the gospels and throughout Christian texts, we are encouraged, when appropriate, to accept our own suffering and even to share the suffering of others. But we are not to leave others in their suffering or to decide for them that their suffering should not be relieved. What we find missing in Hauerwas's discussion of suffering is a distinction between the first person and the second person. Suffering in the first person may appropriately be accepted, but the suffering of a second person, the suffering of others, is to be resisted; it is this conviction that grounds our theology of medicine as healing. To reiterate, we may be called to accept our own suffering, but we are not permitted to accept the suffering of others, much less to accept it *for them.* This point is especially important when the topic is prenatal genetics, because a potential person is involved. We may be called to accept our suffering as parents, but are we permitted to accept suffering for the unborn?

Hauerwas believes it is a misuse of medicine to seek to reject suffering or to reject the tragic character of illness. The purpose of medicine is to provide compassionate care.[49] Medicine's misuse,

Hauerwas believes, may ultimately be much more than an attempt to avoid suffering; its true meaning may be that it is an idolatrous rebellion against God. Manipulating reproduction may mark "a refusal of the image of God's creation in our own."[50] Hauerwas's warning is similar to that of Paul Ramsey, who cautions that "the converging lines of action leading to [humanity's] radical self-modification and control of [our] evolutionary future . . . must simply be described as a project for the suicide of the species."[51] Our current efforts at managing reproduction are but a first step in a Godlike venture of constructing a destiny of our own design and making. Such an idolatrous sentiment is echoed in Iris Murdoch's play, *Acastos,* when a character exclaims: "The gods are just ideal pictures of us; we have to get rid of them to realize our own possibilities."[52]

For Ramsey, the human effort to manage reproduction is inspired by our desire to prevent suffering and improve health, but it is a vain aspiration doomed to failure. For in usurping God's providence, as expressed through natural procreation, "the expectation of godhood following" will be disappointed by a "death to the species. . . ."[53] The mystery of reproduction must be replaced by management techniques so that our children will be created in our own rather than in God's image. We will achieve death rather than life, however, because we reject the truth and beauty of God's created order in favor of our sinful (i.e., deadly) will, desire, and power.[54]

While we agree with Ramsey and Hauerwas that medicine and prenatal genetics can be pursued with hubris or greed, we do not see an inevitable or necessary connection between medical or technological intervention and defiance of the God known to us in Christ. We believe the gospels clearly portray a God revealed to us in Jesus, the healer, who intervenes in the course of nature in order to bring nature closer to what God intends it to be and, simultaneously, to relieve human sufferers of pain and illness.[55] We believe that followers of Christ are called to carry out this task, using the technology available to them, including the proper use of prenatal genetics.

Christian faith does not lead us to a categorical rejection of prenatal genetics but to a nuanced, qualified appreciation. In particular, drawing on Hauerwas's insight but insisting on a distinction between the first and second person, we can say that the Christian faith does not encourage us to use prenatal genetics to avoid our own suffering. It does not absolutely prevent us from doing so, but it certainly invites us to consider the possibility of growth through the acceptance rather than the avoidance of our own suffering. So if it is clear that the purpose of a particular genetic procedure is to avoid pain for Christian parents, then their faith at least encourages them to consider accepting the pain, not the procedure.

But on the other hand, if it is clear that the purpose of a prenatal genetic procedure is to avoid the pain of another, potential person, then Christian faith invites us to consider how we may, with the technical means available to us, act in a manner consistent with the healing ministry of Jesus to relieve or prevent suffering.

One of the more startling critiques of prenatal genetics is offered by Gena Corea, who charges that men are now "beyond merely giving spiritual birth in their baptismal-font wombs, beyond giving physical birth with their electronic fetal monitors, their forceps, their knives." She adds this chilling warning: "Now they have their laboratories."[56] The new technologies are the latest attempt by men to fully dominate and control reproduction. In the past, men used religion, but now they use medicine to redefine the meaning of birth and manipulate its outcome. Infant baptism, for instance, "birthed humans into eternal, immortal life,"[57] but with the development of obstetrics and gynecology men have acquired the scientific and practical power "to control woman's procreative power."[58]

We accept the connection Corea sees between the baptism font and the prenatal genetics laboratory. But we reject the notion that both are nothing but expressions of male dominance over women and over the processes of birth. We claim both as media of grace, even though both are so often compromised by the brokenness and pride of those who administer their powers. Nevertheless, both baptismal font and laboratory can be places of healing. Both can be sacramental manifestations of the God who creates through procreation and who heals through our hands.

5

Creation and Procreation: Connecting God with Genetic Processes

Judy called her pastor, Hector, to arrange a quick meeting. "Tom and I have a terrible decision to make, and we need some help," she told him.

When they were together, she explained: "No one at church knows yet, but I'm expecting in about six months. And there's something wrong with the baby." She and Tom both started to cry. "We just got the test results this morning," she continued. "We can't believe that God would let something like this happen."

"And I can't believe God is punishing us," Tom said. "I mean, we're not perfect, and we've had some problems in our marriage, mostly my fault . . . but why would God punish our baby for something I've done. I should be the one getting sick."

Hector listened as Judy began to speak again. "Why is God letting this happen? It just isn't fair. Can't God keep things like this from happening? All my life I have been taught that God is in charge of everything. The genetic counselor explained to us how a tiny genetic problem is going to cause terrible suffering. If God can't fix such a tiny problem, can God do anything? Or doesn't God care about us?"

"We really, really wanted a baby," Tom said. "But why this?"

Women or couples who confront prenatal genetic problems often ask theological questions: Did God cause this problem? Why doesn't God fix it? What does God want us to do?

People who ask these questions expect that their pastor will be willing to explore them, to share the burden of theological searching, and to wait patiently in times of silence, uncertainty, and pain.

These questions have no easy answers. But when these questions are asked, clergy need to be ready to say more than "We don't know the answer." The agnostic "we don't know" is altogether too simple, too quick, too easy, a convenient avoidance of the difficult theological task of ministry. Of course we do not have ready-made, textbook answers to these questions. But we do have something to say. To believe in God *at all* is to believe that there is a Creator of all things, including nascent human life.[1]

The biblical texts affirm that God is the creator of all things, including each individual life. The handiwork of God is displayed equally in vast galaxies and in the tiny details of human embryology. Many clergy today, however, were taught in seminary to disregard the theme of creation or to see it as a distant second in importance behind the theme of redemption. An important task facing theology today is first to recover the centrality of creation as a theological theme and then to explore the meaning of the presence of God the Creator in the intimate deals of our reproductive lives.

When the Christian community gathers for worship, we confess our faith in God the Creator. But when pastors meet with expectant parents to provide theological companionship, they struggle together with the personal dimension of their confession. Can this confession of faith in God as Creator have meaning, not just for the universe in general, but for the life that is being formed within? Does it apply to the creation of life within the pregnant woman? Where is God in human procreation? Where is God when things go wrong?

Our confessions affirm the universal: God is the Creator of heaven and earth. But a universal affirmation of the creative power of God is little comfort or guidance to the woman or couple who want to know where God is to be found in their particular distress. Our general confession, that God is the Creator of heaven and earth, does not tell us what to do with a genetically affected pregnancy.

Should the woman or couple think of God, who creates all things, as the source of the chromosomal or genetic abnormality that has just been reported to them? Could not the great Creator have prevented this disorder? Is the disorder itself part of God's plan, either to punish them for past sins or to enrich them by letting them rise to overcome the distress of the disorder? Must God allow a certain amount of genetic abnormality in order to create? Is God's will accomplished or defied if they intervene in the course of the pregnancy?

These are the theological questions that women or couples who are undergoing genetic testing are likely to raise in conversation with clergy. In order to be prepared to offer theological companionship, clergy need to reconsider the biblical and traditional understanding of God as Creator, especially the theological understanding of God involved in the human procreative process. But the biblical and traditional texts are not enough, for the traditional writers never had to consider the possibility of technological intervention in the genetic processes of reproduction, nor did they have the contemporary sciences as a window upon the creation and thus as an aid to a theological understanding of God's creative action. They were not able to wonder how God might be understood as creating life on earth, including individual human lives, through genetic processes of mutation and recombination.

Therefore, we begin this chapter by reconsidering the biblical texts related to God and procreation. But we must move on from them to a contemporary theological perspective on the relationship between God and procreation, seeking always to be informed by the growing scientific understandings of the genetic processes that are involved in human procreation.

Biblical Perspectives on Procreation

Many clergy in ministry today were taught in seminary to think that creation is very much a secondary theme in the biblical tradition, ancillary at best to the primary theme of history, of exodus, and especially of the salvation that is mediated through the life and death of Jesus Christ.

Very recently, this view of the biblical tradition has been challenged by theological and biblical scholars. Perhaps the single strongest motivating factor in this reconsideration has been the rise of environmental awareness, and especially the criticism that the church's theology over recent centuries laid the foundation for the contemporary crisis of environmental degradation. Newer movements in biblical scholarship have reclaimed creation and ecological themes in the biblical tradition. Once again, the church recognizes that the Bible speaks of God as the Creator of a good and beautiful creation. Genesis 1 and Genesis 2:4bff are the most familiar biblical creation accounts, but the motif of creation permeates the Psalms, the Wisdom literature, and the Prophets. In the writings of the early Christian church, creation is a less explicit theme than it is in the Hebrew writings. But the Christian biblical writers presupposed that their audiences were grounded in the Hebrew texts.

The recovery of awareness of the biblical theme of creation is important and encouraging. However, this recovery to date has been characterized by two significant omissions. First, contemporary theology has largely ignored the biblical theme of healing and Jesus' identity as a healer. In the synoptic gospels, Jesus is portrayed consistently and predominantly as a healer, as one who acts on nature, specifically on the human body, in order to alter the natural course of events in the progression of disease. This theme has been largely overlooked in theology since the Enlightenment. Its recovery is necessary if Christian theology is to respond, not just to genetics, but to many concerns about human health and its relationship to salvation. A Christian theological assessment of disease, as a condition of nature harmful to humans and inconsistent with the intentions of the Creator, is grounded in these texts which portray Jesus as acting in the name of God to heal disease.

The recovery of the biblical theme of creation has suffered from a second omission. The text of Genesis, at least, focuses far more attention on procreation than on the creation of the cosmos or the planet.

Of course, the familiar opening chapters of Genesis are about the grandeurs of the cosmos as creation, but the chapters that follow are devoted not to the cosmos but to procreation, infertility, conception, birth order of twins, and the pains and blessings that surround such events. Our contemporary recovery of creation has not yet included a recovery of procreation. When we survey the broad scope of biblical texts, we see portrayed a great and glorious God who creates heaven and earth, but who is nevertheless deeply implicated in the details of individual lives, in particular in the human reproductive process. The problem of human infertility and of God's role in resolving it receives a far greater share of attention in the text of Genesis than does God's role in creating the vast, general creation.

Throughout the Hebrew writings, God is presented as One who interacts with individual circumstances in order to achieve God's purposes in the human reproductive process. Human fertility is a persistent theme in Genesis and reappears as a concern in 1 Samuel in the story of Hannah's conception and the birth of Samuel. This motif continues in the writings of the early Church with the story of Elizabeth's unexpected conception and birth of John the Baptizer. Even the story of Mary's conception and the birth of Jesus, the tradition of the virgin birth which has proved so problematic in Christian theology, is perhaps best understood within this centuries-old tradition of miraculous conceptions. A common motif is found in each story: The power of God brings the blessing of conception, which is followed by the birth of a person who is especially important to the unfolding of God's purposes.

Not only conception, but human embryological development is the arena of God's creative splendor, according to the Hebrew texts. In our opening chapter, we noted Psalm 139:13–14:

> For it was you who formed my inward parts;
> you knit me together in my mother's womb.
> I praise you, for I am fearfully and wonderfully made.
> Wonderful are your works;
> that I know very well.
> My frame was not hidden from you,
> when I was being made in secret,

intricately woven in the depths of the earth.
Your eyes beheld my unformed substance.

In this text, the writer describes God as One who plays a role in the psalmist's own fetal development, forming the organs and attaching the limbs, observing and guiding a process that to the ancient Hebrews was no doubt wholly shrouded in mystery. Two themes are striking. One is the power of the Creator to do what we cannot even imagine, namely, to fashion a baby. The second is the intimacy of divine involvement. The language of the psalm is not general or all-encompassing, though certainly the writer was affirming that God creates all human beings (indeed, all organisms) through these same mysterious processes. But what is striking is the intimacy: "I was being made." The great Creator of all is involved in the formation of the individual person.

In Genesis, the first humans beings are commanded to multiply and fill the earth. Human procreation is thus taken out of the realm of the merely natural and placed also in the realm of command, obedience, and faithful, intentional action. Today, as the human population of the planet approaches six billion, many of us have come to see that this is a command that must no longer be obeyed literally; in fact, we see today a command to limit population. But for both the Genesis text and for us today, human procreation is in the realm of command and intention, not merely in the realm of nature or of the spontaneous.

Throughout the Bible, procreation is seen as a blessing and sterility as a curse. Stories of the miraculous conceptions of Sarah, Rachel, Hannah, Elizabeth, and Mary are accounts of God's gracious involvement. The Bible portrays a God who is cosmic in majesty, yet intimately merciful. Even the details of human reproduction and illness are dimensions of God's creative and redemptive acts. Sarah's infertility, for instance, reflects God's punishment, but ultimately she is healed and gives birth to a child (Genesis 18). In other biblical stories, however, the cause of infertility remains unknown or unexplained, but typically God relieves the infertile women from their plight.

Likewise, there are biblical stories where God sends sickness as a form of judgment (see 2 Kings 5 and Acts 13), but most often the causes of illness remain unknown. From a biblical perspective, illness is a result of divine acts or of natural or supernatural forces beyond human understanding or control. Consequently, healing must also originate with some form of divine intervention or consent. God is normally depicted as a healer in the biblical literature, and healing itself is understood as a redemptive act or dimension of salvation. The Bible proclaims God as the One who gives the blessing of both childbirth and healing, the author of life and death (Rom. 14:8), and source of good and evil (Isa. 45:7).

The biblical writers recognized that human procreation and health played important roles in God's intentions for creation. Often, however, God's ends or purposes remained hidden from the human actors, deep within God's unfathomable will, power, and providence. As a mark of divine sovereignty, distinct limits were imposed on human beings for controlling reproduction or preventing disease. Although the Bible proclaims a belief that God is guiding creation to a final consummation, the details of that end, as well as our role in achieving it, remain hidden in the mystery of judgment and grace. Birth, suffering, and death, in short, are unmanageable graces or givens that lie solely within God's creative and redemptive prerogatives and that therefore surpass any human efforts to control, manipulate, or prevent.

The biblical texts present disease, healing, infertility, conception, and human procreation not just as human concerns, but as concerns for God, involving God's creative power. In many cases, God acts to overcome infertility, but not always, and so it would be premature to conclude that the biblical texts generally support the view that infertility is a disease (as we have defined disease), although certain texts suggest this. More safely, we can say that in human procreation, according to the biblical texts from Hebrew and Christian writers, human beings experience and participate in the creative power of God, expressed in the intimate details of sexuality and childbirth.

The God of the biblical writers is not an indifferent artisan or distant force. God does not fashion or give birth to creation and then walk away from what is created. We human beings are not created by an unnamed, unsympathetic, unmoved deity, but by the God of Abraham and Sarah, Rebekkah and Isaac, Jacob and Leah and

Rachel. The God of the biblical tradition and the God of Christian worship is personal, intimately involved in the details of human life, including the process of reproduction.

Today, we have a much more sophisticated understanding of human reproduction than the biblical or traditional writers could have imagined. Whereas they saw fetal development as a great mystery, we are beginning to understand how genes instruct cells to structure our bodies and brains. Biblical writers were baffled by disease, whether acquired or congenital. We now understand that illness can be transmitted through bacteria or viruses, and that tiny errors in the genetic code can cause pain and early death. They were powerless to alter or prevent the genetic traits of individuals, while we are on the threshold of exerting greater control over our destinies.

More to the point, where they could only pray, we can act. The great danger is that we will act without praying, that we will seduce ourselves into believing that when we know *how* to intervene, we will know *when* to intervene, and to *what end* we should intervene. With all our extensive knowledge and technical sophistication, we rarely ponder the theological significance of reproduction, health, and healing. A sense of sacredness should envelop the process of procreation, and from this sense of God's immediate and particular presence should arise our conviction that there are indeed profound moral restraints, which arise because we believe that in sexual reproduction God is working in us to create new human life.

But how are we to connect the activity of God with genetic processes, in light of recent scientific understandings? How far can we go in understanding God to be creating through genetic mutation, recombination, and natural selection? How is God's creativity expressed in the media of genes and proteins and sketched out on no less vast a canvas that the evolution of life on earth?

Creation and Procreation Today

Biblical texts connect God with procreation. But does theology today offer any help at all to expectant women or couples, especially when they are undergoing prenatal genetic testing? This is a question raised provocatively by James Gustafson throughout his *Ethics from a Theocentric Perspective*. He refers to genetic abnormalities to illustrate the practical and ethical significance of basic theological questions, such as how we see the relationship between God and nature. For example, he refers to prenatal diagnosis of "defective" genes as a fact of life with which theological ethics must now come to terms.[2]

Gustafson even uses this question to challenge the theology of Jürgen Moltmann: "I invite the reader to see how far he or she would get making a choice about an induced abortion in light of [Moltmann's] theology and ethics."[3]

Even though it was not Moltmann's purpose in writing *The Theology of Hope* to answer this question, it may be a fair question, not just for Moltmann but for all contemporary theology. To what extent does any of our contemporary theology shed light on the theological legitimacy of a therapeutic abortion? Does Gustafson's own theology help us?

One of the great strengths of Gustafson's writing is his insistence that God, rather than humanity, must be the defining center of value. In other words, he advocates a theocentric rather than an anthropocentric perspective. He argues against the anthropocentric tendencies he sees in modern ethics, secular and religious. He maintains that when contemporary religious ethicists refer to God, their "God" often serves as a mere extension of human self-centeredness. "God is denied as God; God becomes an instrument in the service of human beings rather than human beings instruments in the service of God."[4]

Against such anthropocentrism, Gustafson claims that God must be acknowledged as the source of values and the One who defines moral obligation, transcending all human purposes or humanly defined ends. God's purposes define the place of humanity in nature. Consequently, we live in the midst of forces that evoke gratitude and respect, as well as fear and awe. Nature "brings us into life and sustains life; it also creates suffering and pain and death."[5]

Through the insight of science and theology (particularly the theology of the Reformed tradition), Gustafson believes we can discern enough of what God is doing in creation to know how to respond. "'God' refers to the power that bears down upon us, sustains us, sets an ordering of relationships, provides conditions of possibilities for human activity and even a sense of direction."[6] While we cannot discern a "final purposiveness in nature," we can perceive sufficient ordering to affirm "that a 'governance' is occurring."[7] Gustafson argues that life itself is made possible by these ordering processes of nature. Any life that would flourish must respect these ordering processes as prerequisites for existence. As an example of an ordering process, Gustafson alludes to genetic conditions that are imperative to normal organic development: "An infant with a particular chromosomal defect will not have the capacities for human development that a genetically normal infant has," he writes. "The biological prerequisite for normal development is not there."[8]

What is unclear about Gustafson's argument is what he means by a "chromosomal defect." Trisomy 21, for instance, is a chromosomal disorder that causes Down's syndrome. It is a "defect" if judged statistically, because it occurs infrequently. It may also be a "defect" if lowered intelligence is used as a standard. On what theocentric basis, however, is this judgment made? On what ground can we affirm that Down's syndrome is "defective" when judged against divine purposes and intentions for creation?

According to Gustafson, God is identified with the natural ordering processes. If true, then it can be argued that in Down's syndrome, or any other "chromosomal defect," an ordering process has gone awry, which is contrary to the Creator's intention. It is also possible, however, to maintain that the Creator intends (for whatever reasons, biological or spiritual, but unknown to us) that a certain percentage of human conceptions be affected with trisomy 21 or other "chromosomal defects." In fact, after insisting that we must consent to the ordering processes of nature, Gustafson intimates that such a defect may be an ordering process: "If a chromosomal defect cannot be corrected, we can consent to it (not merely resign ourselves to it) and participate in the development of a limited natural capacity."[9]

It is important to note a key qualification in Gustafson's argument—"if a chromosomal defect cannot be corrected." What we should consent to, apparently, is defined and thus redefinable by the current limits of our technology, or as Gustafson claims, what "is relative to our knowledge."[10] The horizon of "consent" recedes with technological advance and is not defined theologically or by any apparent moral a priori. Gustafson is offering a tautology (we cannot change what we cannot change) rather than theology (we must not change what God ordains). Or, from an ethical perspective, we are advised to consent only to what we cannot yet control.

When Gustafson goes on to address the meaning of "redeeming grace," he describes it "as redemption from conditions of fatedness, and as redemption from sin."[11] He illustrates both categories by again referring to genetics. As a condition of fatedness, he observes that "many persons suffer from diseases that are genetically transmitted. . . . Medical interventions can manage the symptoms if not cure the causes of some inherited diseases."[12] When such medical intervention is successful, "a form of redemption is occurring."[13]

In regard to redemption from sin, Gustafson notes that we should not feel guilty for conditions we do not cause, then adds: "Unfortunately there are still persons who feel guilt for the birth of a defective child."[14] Ironically, because technology has redefined the ordering processes to which we must consent, parents are becoming increasingly accountable for the genetic health of their offspring. On these grounds it might be argued that the failure to use technologies, such as abortion or in vitro fertilization, is sinful. It is not clear, however, which acts based on the knowledge these technological interventions provide are morally appropriate.

Abortion, for instance, could be inferred as a "form of redemption" in that it is a release from "conditions of fatedness." Yet it could also be construed, from Gustafson, that if the abnormality cannot be corrected, it is a condition of the ordering processes of nature to which we must consent without recourse to abortion. Is aborting a genetically "defective" fetus a failure to consent to nature's ordering? Or is opting not to abort a failure to join in the divine ordering of nature? As already mentioned, as many as 60 percent of all human conceptions occur with chromosomal abnormalities. Over 99 percent of these conceptions fail to implant or abort spontaneously, so that chromosomal abnormalities affect about one in two hundred live births. As we increase our ability to screen for additional abnormalities, would it not be the natural thing to imitate nature and abort them as well? Or is the natural thing to consent to nature and care for a child with limited capacities?

Underlying this theological and moral ambiguity is too great a proximity between God and nature. For while Gustafson is brilliantly helpful in his critique of anthropocentrism, the close proximity in Gustafson's thinking between God and nature makes it difficult for us to distinguish the intentions of the Creator from natural processes. His theology is not so much theocentric but nature-centered. On what grounds, then, should we ever reject what nature gives us? From an anthropocentric view, a severe genetic disorder is a human problem that requires a response, including the possibility of abortion. But on Gustafson's God/nature-centered ground, the fitting moral response to a fetus diagnosed with a severe genetic illness or disorder is not clear. So we would pose to Gustafson the very question with which he challenged the ideas of Jürgen Moltmann: "I invite the reader to see how far he or she would get making a choice about an induced abortion in light of this theology and ethics."[15]

Arthur Peacocke maintains a more traditional theistic distinction between God and nature than does Gustafson, arguing that this is an appropriate dualism that must not be surrendered. In current popular thought, there is a trend toward rejecting all dualisms. Many who reject dualism generally are unclear about what they are rejecting specifically. Is it the division between mind and body, humanity and nature, or between God and creation? Peacocke is quite clear about wanting to eliminate all dualisms within creation, but not the distinction between God and nature, claiming that this ontological difference or dualism is foundational to Christian beliefs in creation, incarnation, and redemption. Peacocke insists that "this dualism—God and the world—is the only one that is foundational to Christian thought."[16]

When we distinguish (as does Peacocke) between God and nature, then we must be prepared to deal with a difficult question: How can God be thought of as acting in nature? Any attempt to answer this question for today must begin with nature as described by the sciences. Our focus here is on the biological and genetic processes. How can we think of the God we worship as active in these processes as we have come to understand them through science and even to act upon them through genetic technology? This is a biblical question that requires a contemporary answer, informed by today's biological perspectives.

Contemporary biology is a remarkably fruitful synthesis of Darwinian evolution and genetics. According to contemporary biology, at the genetic level, random mutations and their continuous reshuffling in recombination processes within a breeding population produces great variety in offspring, especially in sexually reproducing organisms. Mutations in genes or new patterns of combinations among genes in offspring mean that offspring may vary significantly among themselves. Some may have lethal combinations of genes, and they will not survive to reproduce. Others may have a new gene or combination of genes that gives them a better chance to survive and to reproduce in their environment. In that case, nature, in the language of Darwinian evolution, selects for survival and reproduction those individual organisms that, by chance, inherit genetic combinations that give them some advantage in the struggle to survive.

Is it possible to think of God acting through a process of chance and natural selection? Many today think that the answer is no: The modern biological synthesis of genetics and evolution wholly explains life on earth in a way that excludes the idea of a divine creator. The influential French biologist Jacques Monod argues that chance alone provides the raw material of the evolutionary process. Therefore, because chance plays the central role in evolution, the process as a whole must be seen as unguided and purposeless. For Monod, the fundamental role of chance excludes the possibility that there is a transcendent cause of evolution. According to Monod, we might believe in God, but we can no longer think this God creates life on earth by acting within the evolutionary process. Not only does evolution not need God; it excludes God.

This is a profoundly serious challenge, not just for our project in this book, but for contemporary Christian theology as a whole. If Monod is unanswered, then Christianity should acknowledge that all its talk about God acting to create, sustain, and renew the biological creation as new creation, is on shaky ground. Very few theologians and philosophers have taken on the task of responding to Monod.[17] If Monod is right, no theological perspective can be brought to bear on the questions of women or couples undergoing prenatal genetic testing. When they ask "Is there any connection whatsoever between the God we worship and the genetic event that is now so distressing to us?" the honest pastor would have to answer no. Genetic events are the result of chance and not in any respect the work of God.

Creationists, of course, challenge Monod by challenging contemporary biology, in particular the theory of evolution and its relationship with genetics. A more promising strategy is to challenge Monod's interpretation of the science. Specifically, is Monod right in holding that chance excludes a divine role? Is it possible to understand genetic chance as compatible with belief in a creator who has a role in how organisms such as us have evolved?

Ironically, many mainstream clergy and the academic theologians who teach them are in functional agreement with Monod: God has nothing to do with matters biological. Such a view is not only a rejection of the biblical tradition; it has deeply disturbing consequences for human life. It separates God from the processes by which we come into existence, thereby permitting us to see these processes and to act on them with total theological disregard, as if what we do does not matter theologically or morally. This demeans the human body, human physicality, human life itself.

Two contemporary theologians, Arthur R. Peacocke and Robert J. Russell, have taken a very different approach. Their response to Monod is helpful in enabling us to reconnect God with biological creation and human procreation. Peacocke regards Monod's views as "one of the strongest and most influential attacks of the century on theism."[18] In response to Monod, Peacocke does not reject Monod's evolutionary biology but challenges the metaphysical (or antitheistic) conclusions Monod draws from science. Randomness or chance at the genetic level does not necessarily mean that the whole evolutionary process is unguided or purposeless, or more precisely, that it lacks the propensity to generate organisms of great complexity. Peacocke argues that, in the natural universe we observe through science, chance at the level of genetic events is balanced by the constraints of natural law or the inherent property of matter to follow statistical laws and to give rise to complex patterns. Chance alone is not creative. "It is the interplay of chance and law which is in fact creative within time, for it is the combination of the two which allows new forms to emerge and evolve."[19] The sort of complexity that we see to such a stunning degree in living organisms does not arise from chance alone, but only from "the interplay and consequences of random processes (in relation to biological outcome) in the lawlike framework of the rules governing change in biological populations in complex environments."[20] Chance is the source of novelty, but the lawlike framework that is inherent in the universe is what makes it possible for this novelty to yield organized complexity.

Where is God in this interplay of chance and law? For Peacocke, God is to be understood as the Creator who endows the universe with its lawlike principles. For science, these lawlike properties are simply given, as inherent properties of the universe. But "this givenness, for a theist, can only be regarded as an aspect of the God-endowed features of the world."[21] God defines the initial properties of the universe. In so doing, God establishes certain propensities toward which the results of chance events will inevitably move, not because they are secretly guided but because they occur within a lawlike framework. By establishing these initial conditions of the universe, God establishes propensities or potentialities for the outcome of the evolutionary process. "Such potentialities a theist must regard as written into creation by the Creator's intention and purpose and must conceive as gradually being actualized by the operation of 'chance' stimulating their coming into existence."[22]

For God to establish inherent propensities or potentialities, however, is not for God to predetermine the universe, to foreordain the evolution of the human species, much less to predetermine that a particular human individual will be born with a particular set of genes. The details of the unfolding of the universe are filled in by chance, even though God has sketched out the general direction and purpose of evolution in advance. God sets the rules of the game "which, as it were, 'load the dice' in favour of life and, once living organisms have appeared, also of increased complexity, awareness, consciousness and sensitivity, with all their consequences."[23] The game may be structured, but each roll of the dice is an event of chance. Genes are composed of random or chance occurrences within intricate structures and causal patterns.

This interplay between chance and purpose, therefore, has personal implications: "In human life we must accept, for the stability of our own mental health and of our faith, that reality has a dimension of chance interwoven with a dimension of causality—and that through such interweaving we come to be here and new forms of existence can arise."[24] In this view, God is involved in the biological evolution of our species and even our own reproduction, but God does not determine the precise outcome or the exact set of genes we inherit. Peacocke argues against determinism in both its philosophical and theological forms. For God to be involved in these processes is not to remove the element of chance but to orchestrate it toward a larger whole.

Peacocke's proposals seem to have an immediate attraction. They appear to remove God from any possibility of blame when genetic problems cause suffering. In Peacocke's view, God determines the basic physical properties of the universe, including the rules of physics that genes and proteins (which are physical entities) must obey. In so doing, God establishes the propensity of the universe for complex organisms. But God does not determine specific genetic events; these are the result of chance. When these events lead to illness or suffering, God may be thought of as regretting the pain, perhaps even as sharing the suffering, but not as causing it. We may ask Peacocke, however, whether God is to be blamed for setting up such a universe. Could God not have made a different, possibly even a better universe, especially one with a better history of life on earth, one not characterized by so much death, and one in which infants with genetic defects do not have to pay part of the price of genetic evolution?

Such a creation is filled with both wonder and pain, and a God who is the author of its wonder must also be recognized in relationship to its pain. For Peacocke, the clue to understanding God's association with the pain of creation is found in the cross of Jesus Christ. "Jesus then is, as it were, a bearer of God's pain, the pain of the creative process," which on the cross is "concentrated into a point of unique intensity and transparency for us all to perceive."[25]

Because of this distinction between God and the world, Peacocke recognizes the difference between God's creative intentions and their achievement in creation. Since God is working in and through natural processes, some of which are characterized by chance, God does not control the outcome of each particular situation. And since God does not control the outcome, we cannot infer that it is exactly what God intends. Chromosomal or genetic abnormalities, for example, are not directly caused or intended by God, but are accepted as the inevitable cost of creating through biological processes. As Peacocke has written:

> The chance disorganization of the growing human embryo that leads to the birth of a defective human being and the chance loss of control of cellular multiplication that appears as a cancerous tumour are individual and particular results of that same interplay of "chance" and "law" that enabled and enables life at all. . . . Even God cannot have one without the other.[26]

Or as John Polkinghorne observes:

> If love implies the acceptance of vulnerability by endowing the world with an independence which will find its way through the shuffling operations of chance rather than by rigid divine control . . . then the world that such a God creates will look very much like the one in which we live, not only in its beautiful structure but also in its evolutionary blind alleys and genetic malfunctions.[27]

If God is to achieve certain purposes for creation, then biological processes occur in an unpredictable and imperfect interplay between law and chance. God does not intend any fetus to develop genetic abnormalities, but undesirable disorders will inevitably occur in the reproductive process. Neither God nor parents are to be blamed when genetic problems occur.

Peacocke's work is highly significant as a response to Monod. It is also a very attractive position for pastors who are wrestling with the question of the activity of God the Creator in relation to genetic problems. Essentially, Peacocke enables us to say that God has a role in genetic processes: first, by establishing the lawlike framework in which all natural processes occur, and thus in working through genetic process to create complex creatures such as ourselves; and second, by enfolding into God's own being the suffering that creatures experience when genetic processes lead to illness and pain. In Peacocke's view, however, God is not so closely tied to genetic processes that God should be thought of as the cause of any genetic event. Such events are to be regarded as chance, not as divine will. If Peacocke is correct, then when pastors are asked "Did God cause our baby's prenatal disease?" they can reply that God creates through genetic processes, but God does not cause—and God certainly does not intend—any genetic disease.

Is Peacocke correct? Has he accurately portrayed the relationship between God and genetic events? Very recently, an important (though highly exploratory) counterproposal has been made by Robert J. Russell, building upon but significantly revising Peacocke's work.[28] A problem with Peacocke, according to Russell, is that his view fails to show how God can be seen as acting in specific, contemporary genetic events. For Peacocke, God's direct action is confined to endowing the physical universe with its propensities, via its lawlike structures, toward the eventual evolution of complex organisms. This is an important but highly limited role for God, according to Russell, for it confines God's direct activity to the creation of the universe, making God a very important first cause but largely irrelevant to the subsequent unfolding of the creation. In this sense, according to Russell, Peacocke's position unintentionally resembles deism.[29]

Does God guide the evolutionary process *as it unfolds,* influencing it toward the evolution of conscious creatures, not just by initially establishing conditions that favor their appearance but by acting directly *at the genetic level* to influence the direction of biological complexity? Russell thinks that it is possible for a theist to answer yes to this question in a way that is fully compatible with contemporary science. He bases his position on the relationship between genetic events, which occur at the molecular level in DNA, and subatomic or quantum events. Unlike the objects that we deal with in everyday life, genes are molecules, structured by bonds between atoms such as hydrogen and carbon. Genes are altered or mutated when atomic bonds are altered, and this process of making or breaking atomic bonds within the DNA structure is itself a quantum process.

For evolution to occur, there must be variation or differences among individual organisms. Underlying the differences among organisms are genetic differences, and so genetic variation plays a key role in evolution. This is where Russell focuses his attention. The close relationship between any organism and its genes allows subatomic or quantum events to have enormous consequences in the everyday world of human beings. We know that genetic mutations can have profound effects on the health of a human being or another organism. Quantum events, to the extent that they are involved in genetic mutations, can have indirect but great significance at the everyday level of organisms. Likewise, quantum events can have great significance in the history of evolution. Evolution requires mutations, and inasmuch as quantum events explain genetic mutations, quantum events are profoundly important for the amount of novelty in the evolutionary process.

How does this affect our understanding of the relationship between God and genetic mutations? The answer, Russell observes, depends on how we understand the meaning of indeterminacy at the quantum level. Russell argues that it is plausible to interpret quantum physics as an indication that nature is fundamentally indeterminant. That is to say, at the most basic level, nature provides a set of causes that are necessary, but not sufficient, to produce a quantum event. Some philosophers and scientists disagree, of course, and argue for a deterministic interpretation of quantum physics. In their view, the causes that nature provides are both necessary and sufficient, although they may not be knowable. Russell, however, argues for the interpretation he terms "ontological indeterminacy," according to which *"there is no sufficient underlying causal process."*[30]

If this interpretation of quantum physics is defensible, then the theist can add, without contradiction from the sciences, that God can be thought of as acting within nature by acting in quantum events. Seeing God as acting in quantum events does not make God a cause like other causes within the universe; it does not reduce God to a force, a physical entity, or a prior event in a causal sequence. But precisely because quantum events do not result from a closed causal sequence, they lack sufficient explanation according to science; and thus science leaves open the possibility that God, acting together with nature, is their sufficient explanation. Russell comments:

> If my interpretation is correct, it allows us to conceive of God as acting in nature without violating the laws of nature, since according to these laws, nature alone is insufficient to determine what actually will happen in the future. Nature alone provides a set of necessary (formal, material) but not sufficient (efficient) causes. If that is true, we might be in a position to argue that God provides the sufficient condition for the actual outcome.[31]

We do not usually think that our health depends on quantum events or that God may have a role to play in our health by acting through the quantum level. There is a relationship, however, among quantum events, genetic mutations, and the health of the organism. It is this relationship that makes this point theologically significant, according to Russell. Ordinarily, no one but a physicist pays attention to events at the subatomic level. Even though we ourselves are made up of such events, the effect of any single subatomic event is lost, as it were, in a vast ocean of such events, which averages out the significance of any single quantum event. That is, unless such an event is the determinative factor in a genetic mutation. For when a quantum event causes a genetic mutation, and the mutation expresses itself in human health or sickness, the consequences of the quantum event can be truly significant.

In this way, Russell argues, it is possible to say theologically, without contradiction by contemporary science, that God acts in genetic events, thereby guiding the evolutionary process. God does this not merely by establishing its lawlike framework at the beginning of the universe, as Peacocke suggests, but by inducing mutations favorable toward God's intended outcomes. God, we believe, intends the evolution of creatures capable of self-consciousness, freedom, and communion with God. Toward this end, Russell asserts, God acts constantly in nature to bring quantum events to a sufficient determination of their outcome, thereby triggering intended genetic mutation events that help the evolutionary process toward God's chosen goals.

Traditional theologians have often insisted that God's role in nature be understood as both universal and as particular or individual. Mary Potter Engel quotes John Calvin, for example, as speaking of the "universal providence of God as special,"[32] through which God guides the universe as a whole and yet cares for each creature. Engel comments: "By this he [Calvin] means that God takes special care at each moment of the workings of nature to move each thing as the principal cause. Everything, then, is a miracle,"[33] regardless of whether it appears unusual or miraculous to us.[34]

The theological advantage of such a position is obvious: It allows us to say that God acts in history (meaning here evolutionary history) and to mean something specific by our statement. It also allows us to say that God is involved in our own conception and in the conception and the genetic health of our offspring, and once again to mean something quite specific. God, we can affirm, is at work in the quantum events in our own bodies, which lead to our production of the sex cells that give rise to our children. Here, procreation and creation are profoundly linked. Russell's proposal, if valid, does justice to the biblical tradition.

But the disadvantage is equally obvious, for if God is this directly involved in genetic processes, then how do we excuse God from blame when these processes lead to disease and pain? If God can determine the quantum events that trigger genetic outcomes such as the mutation of a base in a DNA sequence, why does God not alter the few base pairs that we now know are implicated in some diseases, such as sickle-cell anemia? Some will prefer Peacocke's proposal, because it seems to protect God from such direct involvement and thus from blame. Russell, however, raises an important concern about Peacocke's view: If the universe is in fact open to divine action at the quantum level, and through the quantum level to the genetic level, and ultimately to human health, must we not blame God if God does not act at all in this way?[35]

Recent theologians, overwhelmed by the magnitude of evil in the twentieth century, have tended to distance God from natural and historical events, thereby protecting God from blame. But we protect God from blame at the cost of distancing God from specific events, natural or historical. A God who does nothing is blamed for nothing. Russell's proposal, by contrast, should not be rejected because it heightens God's vulnerability to blame. Any good theology that dares to be specific will do this. Indeed, Russell's proposal opens a way for theologians to rethink several core Christian doctrines, including salvation, the relationship between forgiveness and healing, and the resurrection. For too long, theologians have said that God acts in creating and redeeming all things, without struggling to say *how* God acts.

The views of Peacocke and Russell need to be seen as helpful contributions to our ongoing inquiries into a central religious question of our age: namely, how can we understand God as the Creator of the universe as we are coming to understand the universe through contemporary science? In particular, how can we understand God as creating the organic and genetic processes that surround human procreation? This is the painful question that is at stake when expectant parents ask us, "Did God make our baby sick?"

6

The Presence of God in Pain

Cindy and Tim knew from the time they met that abortion always would be wrong for them. Any pregnancy is a gift from God, they believed.

But when they received Cindy's amniocentesis test results, Tim began to wonder: Surely this is an exception. For a few days he kept his questions to himself, partly because Cindy seemed so sure that an abortion was never the right thing to do, and partly because Tim saw himself as abandoning his own moral principles and wanting to take the easy way out.

Finally he told Cindy about his thoughts. "Remember what the genetic counselor said," he reminded Cindy. "This is a painful condition. How can we let a life continue when it will only be a life of pain?"

"Of course we'll suffer," Cindy said. "But being a Christian means being willing to accept suffering."

"But that's just it. It's one thing for you and me to suffer. But how can we let this happen to our baby?"

Cindy answered: "I would do anything to keep this from happening to our baby. Anything except end the pregnancy. That's worse than the disease."

In the last chapter, we asked whether we should think of God acting in any way to cause genetic changes, including genetic conditions that give rise to disease. In this chapter, we want to ask the opposite question: Is God *affected* in any way by disease, especially genetic diseases that can be diagnosed prenatally? How does God respond to the disease, anguish, and pain that a genetic condition can bring, both for the patient and for the family?

This is a theological question with direct ethical implications. Most Christians believe that our actions should conform to God's actions—not that we imitate God in every respect, but that what we take to be God's response to a situation is the most important consideration in determining our own response. It makes a great deal of difference, therefore, whether we see God responding with indifference or compassion. Not only are we comforted by the thought that God responds with compassion, but we are challenged to respond compassionately ourselves. Throughout this chapter, the relationship between theology and ethics will be a persistent subtheme.

Understanding where God is to be found in reference to human suffering is important for yet another reason, beyond our comfort or our ethical guidance. If we know where God is located in the situation of anguish, then we will know better how to find ourselves in communion with God. A persistent theme in Christian thought about suffering is that through suffering, we may grow into greater awareness of the presence of God. This is not guaranteed; some suffering simply overwhelms us. Nor is it a justification for suffering; God does not abuse us into a submissive love. But it is a possibility, one that becomes all the more accessible if we know where to look for God when anguish and disease confront us.

We want to acknowledge at the outset that we cannot define suffering.[1] Its meaning must be broad, encompassing physical pain, social humiliation, psychological anguish, and theological despair. Its causes are equally broad, arising from physical wounds, poverty, sexual abuse, betrayed relationships, grief, ridicule, violations of rights, viral pathogens, and genetic malfunctions. It is profoundly personal, even subjectively individualistic, for no one can confirm or deny that another suffers. And yet suffering is ultimately social, for we suffer because of others, in the eyes of others, and often abandoned by others, but sometimes in companionship with others. When we attempt a definition of suffering, we quickly discover that "on analysis suffering turns out to be an extremely elusive subject."[2]

In this chapter, our attention is turned primarily to suffering that arises because of the diseases that have a genetic basis. But the suffering that comes to those affected by a genetic condition is far more complex than the physical pain that the condition itself might cause. They suffer socially, not just genetically or physically. Should we presume, for example, that retardation (when caused by a chromosomal abnormality) is suffering in and of itself, or that it is the primary source of suffering for those affected? "No doubt, like everyone, the retarded suffer. . . . But the question is whether they suffer from being retarded. . . . It is possible that they are in fact taught by us that they are decisively disabled, and thus learn to suffer."[3] Social contempt may be a far greater cause of suffering for some than chromosomal abnormality. Often we project onto those with disabilities the pain we think we would feel if we had a disability.

Our task, therefore, borders on the impossible, for we are trying to do no less than locate the transcendent in precise relationship to the indefinable. Such a task would be impossible were it not for the cross, which for Christian theology fixes the location of God at the center, at the focal point, of creation's suffering. It is the cross of Jesus Christ that plays "a decisive role in the way that God participates in our suffering."[4] This chapter, therefore, is a theology of the cross, particularly the cross and the suffering that comes from disease, especially genetic disease.

The Suffering God

Christian theology in the mid-twentieth century has been riveted to the question of suffering, largely because of the enormity of human suffering during the two world wars. This focus is to be found in virtually all the schools and movements of contemporary theology and among writers from Asia, Africa, and Latin America as well as Europe and North America. Process theologians have made God and suffering one of their central themes, while trinitarian theologian Jürgen Moltmann declares that no less than "all Christian theology and all Christian life is basically an answer to the question which Jesus asked as he died."[5]

Common to virtually all contemporary approaches to theology is a rejection of the classic axiom that lies at the foundation of most Western understandings of God—namely, that God is above suffering and thus must be said to be incapable of suffering. "The question about God and the question about suffering are a joint, a common question. And they only find a common answer."[6] God is now seen by most contemporary theologians not primarily as the one who permits or even sends us our pain, but as the universal bearer of the world's pain.

Most contemporary theologians argue that the capacity to love is at bottom fundamentally the same thing as the capacity to suffer, and it would therefore not be possible to say that God loves the creation without also saying that God is capable of suffering with the creation. A loving God is a vulnerable God, vulnerable to the pain of sympathy, "taken in its literal sense of *sympatheia*—'suffering with.'"[7] Christians who are willing to use personal language and to speak of God as loving should recognize "that a loving God must be a sympathetic and therefore suffering God."[8]

Of all the varied ways in which contemporary theology has sought to understand the relationship between God and suffering, the one we find most satisfying is a trinitarian approach, adopted by many theologians but perhaps most significantly associated with Jürgen Moltmann. This approach not only rests more solidly than others in the biblical and the traditional creedal documents of Christianity; it provides the most vivid account of how suffering affects God and thus how we may hope in God. Our task here will be to draw out the insights of Moltmann and other recent trinitarian theologians and to ask what help they can give us in understanding God's presence in genetic testing, diagnosis, decision, and perhaps in death.

The central affirmation of the trinitarian approach to the question of divine suffering is that the one who dies on the cross is the Christ, the second person of the Trinity. Most often, earlier theologians identified the one who dies as a human being: either they saw Jesus as merely human or claimed that the humanity but not the divinity of Christ actually suffers and dies. In either case, it is humanity, not God, who suffers. God, after all, is traditionally considered to be above suffering, and therefore the one who suffers on the cross cannot be God.

However, for recent trinitarian theology, the subject of the suffering is the second person of the Trinity or the Christ, who together with the first person of the Trinity and with the Holy Spirit shares in the communal life of the Trinity, which is God. The triune God experiences the event of the cross and suffers its effects, but each person of the Trinity does so distinctly. Using the traditional names for the first and second persons of the Trinity, Moltmann suggests how we might see them experiencing the cross distinctly: "The Son suffers in his love being forsaken by the Father as he dies. The Father suffers in his love the grief of the death of the Son."[9] In the very center of the triune life, God suffers the event of the cross as pain, abandonment, and grief.

This is an astounding and controversial claim, for it challenges not only the classic axiom that God is above suffering, but it distinguishes the persons of the Trinity in a way that most theologians have considered inappropriate. In fact, according to another axiom of Western Christianity, the works or actions of the Trinity are not to be divided among the persons, as if one creates, another redeems, and yet another sanctifies. According to this axiom, the entire Trinity creates, redeems, and sanctifies; and Moltmann, of course, would not dispute that principle. Nevertheless, he suggests that, in the redeeming work of the cross, for example, the entire Trinity acts but each person of the Trinity acts in a distinguishable way. For instance, we would not say that the first person of the Trinity dies, or even (strictly speaking) that God dies; but we must say that Christ dies. By insisting on these trinitarian distinctions, Moltmann shows how theology can speak of God and suffering, even of God and death, without falling into nonsense by saying, for instance, "God dies." We cannot use nontrinitarian theistic language to speak coherently about God and death, for then we can only speak of the death of God. By contrast, trinitarian theological language permits us to say that Christ—one of the persons of the Trinity—suffers and dies, and thus that death is taken up into the Trinity itself. "Jesus' death cannot be understood 'as the death of God,' but only as death *in* God."[10]

In the event of the cross, God opens up the very being of God to embrace all human suffering within the divine life. For Moltmann, this is the ground of the hope of salvation. "Only if all disaster, forsakenness by God, absolute death, the infinite curse of damnation and sinking into nothingness is in God himself, is community with this God eternal salvation, infinite joy, indestructible election and divine life."[11] For salvation to be possible, "God must contain the whole uproar of history within" God's own life.[12] God becomes associated with the "uproar of history" so that we might become associated with the community of the triune life.

In Moltmann's theology, the event of the cross is seen in relation to the experience of innocent suffering that results from social and political oppression and from systematic violence. Can the cross also be seen in relation to the destruction of nature, whether by nuclear catastrophe or by the slower process of environmental degradation? Can the cross also be understood in relation to human health and disease, in relation to genetic disorders and to their consequences? More broadly, can the event of the cross be understood as *an event with significance for nature* and not just for human history or for human political struggles? Is nature encompassed in this event? Is nature, too, taken up into the life of the triune God?

In his theological engagement with the crucifixion narratives, Moltmann is right to call attention to Jesus' cry of forsakenness as central to the theological meaning of the event. It is this cry, so difficult for all traditional theologians to interpret, that discloses for us the trinitarian depth of the event. But another dimension of the event of the cross, which Moltmann almost wholly ignores, is also difficult for our theology to comprehend. That is the dimension of sheer physicality, of pain, of the destruction of a human body through the agonizing procedure of crucifixion. Moltmann, again, is quite right to criticize the tendency to beautify the cross as jewelry, to place it between candles or among roses. "The symbol of the cross in the church points to the God who was crucified not between two candles on an altar, but between two thieves in the place of the skull, where the outcasts belong outside the gates of the city."[13] The unadorned cross is unfashionable throughout, but its least fashionable dimension—that which never fails to embarrass us, that which is included last if at all in our theology—is that the one who died there was physically broken, afflicted with pain, and made to die in weakness and agony.

How can we begin to understand the theological significance of the physical pain and brokenness of Christ on the cross?[14] What possible theological significance can there be, not just in the dying, the political rejection, the social humiliation, even the theological forsakenness, but also in the physical pain? Why is it not enough that Christ should die, rejected by the political powers, the religious leaders, his closest friends, and even by the one he called "Abba"? What theological meaning is there to the protracted physical pain of Christ's dying? We must look for an answer in relation to the incarnation itself, in relation to Christ's taking on our full humanity, including our vulnerability to sickness, brokenness, pain, and dissipation of strength. These human vulnerabilities are but the full depth of incarnation. Traditional Christian doctrine, centered in the definition of Chalcedon, holds that Jesus Christ is fully human, fully assuming human nature—including, as we must say today, the human genome. It is our nature as genetic creatures, which we share in common with all other biological organisms, that is taken up or assumed by Christ in the incarnation. Genetic processes and all their vulnerabilities are taken up into the relationship between humanity and God that is established in Jesus Christ.

But the theological meaning of the physical suffering of the crucified must also be discovered in relation to Christ's identity as the healer. The Gospels consistently identify Jesus Christ as a healer. It is far more than cruel irony that the healer is bruised, with bones broken and bodily functions intentionally brought to a painful end. The fact that the healer suffers physical pain akin to sickness teaches us something profound about the relationship between healing and suffering.

If the theological meaning of the physical sufferings of Christ on the cross must be understood in relationship to the incarnation and to the identity of Christ as healer, it must also be understood in relation to the resurrection. The resurrection of Christ and the anticipation of a general resurrection must be seen, of course, not as the literalistic resuscitation of a dead body for a second period of life, not as the mythological dying and rising of a god, and especially not as the annual renewal of nature in early spring. Resurrection must be seen as nothing less than the transfiguration of physical existence, a breaking of all predictable cycles, so that nature itself is capable of everlasting relationship with God. In this everlasting relationship, nature remains as creature, distinct from God, not absorbed into God's being or memory.

It is no mere coincidence that in Western Christian theology since the Enlightenment, these four themes—incarnation, physical suffering on the cross, healing, and resurrection—have all been vague and understated in most theological discussions, almost as if this group of doctrines were seen as an embarrassment, as a naive and primitive legacy of the less-sophisticated age of the early church. However, more careful reflection reveals that what once was thought to be intellectual advance over more-primitive forms of thought is not without its own costs, for Western Christian theology has largely lost its ability to connect God with nature, with biological processes such as genetics, with sickness and healing, and with the hope that nature finally will not be discarded but itself will be redeemed. Incarnation, healing, physical suffering on the cross, and resurrection are inextricably connected themes which appear to stand or, most often, fall together. Most theology since the Enlightenment either finds these themes unworthy of serious discussion or treats them as loose symbols (with resurrection, for instance, becoming the symbol of new beginnings and happy endings). Alternatively, it dephysicalizes and spiritualizes them, so that resurrection becomes the immorality of an unnatural psyche rather than the transfiguration of our natures.

In the next section, we will consider the relationship between healing and the suffering of the cross. In later chapters, we will explore these themes in relation to resurrection.

The Crucified Healer

At a strictly literary level, it is at least profoundly ironic that in the Gospels, the healer is physically mutilated. Simone Weil finds this same ironic twist in the story of Prometheus in the Greek dramatic tragedy of Aeschylus:

> From the moment that Prometheus is alone, he has an explosion of pain which leaves no doubt as to the carnal character of his suffering. . . . He had pity and received no pity. . . . The Greeks were haunted by the thought that caused a saint of the Middle Ages to weep: the thought that Love is not loved. . . . Prometheus is a physician who cannot find a cure for himself.[15]

Weil regards this as a pre-Christian intimation of the truth of the cross.

In the physical sufferings of the crucified, we see at the center of Christian faith a narrative of the destruction of the body: a deliberate brutalization, the infliction of wounds, the immobilization of the body by the nails, the inability of the blood and lungs to support metabolic processes, the loss of body fluids, the loss of consciousness, and the loud wail of anguish. These are conditions not unlike the pain and the disruption of the body that some genetic diseases can cause, which may immobilize, limit cognitive functions, and undermine other body functions, leading to pain and death.

The sufferer on the cross is the same one who responds again and again in compassion when surrounded by the physical pain of others. The Jesus of the synoptic Gospels is above all a healer. Jesus did not avoid the sick and ill. The distinctive marks of his ministry were revealed in acts where "the blind receive their sight, the lame walk, the lepers are cleansed, the deaf hear, the dead are raised" (Luke 7:22; see also 4:18). Healing is central to Jesus' identity and thus to the meaning of the salvation he announces. Of course, healing was often accompanied by the forgiveness of sins, but theology has attached so much importance to the forgiveness of sins that it has largely overlooked the healings, especially the fact that the healings seem often to have occurred without any reference to sin.

But how are we to understand the relationship between the Christ who heals and the Christ who suffers? Is the relationship purely coincidental? Could Christ be seen as *the Healer*, as Healing and Salvation itself, as the definitive revelation of the true meaning of healing in relation to salvation, if Christ did not suffer? It is only in the cross that we see the true meaning of healing as salvation, for only on the cross do we see both the cost of healing and its true location in relation to power and vulnerability.

The suffering of the healer on the cross reveals that healing does not come through power alone, but through power that lets itself become vulnerable to the pain it relieves and to the destruction it overcomes. In the pain of the healer on the cross, we see that true healing is willing to accept for itself the pain of the sufferer, that pain is not so much eliminated as willingly transferred from the one who suffers to the one who heals. Although healing is an *action* of power, it is also a *suffering* of vulnerability. The one who acted in power to heal is now suffering in weakness. Some at the cross mocked him, saying "He saved others; himself he cannot save," surely referring to his physical pain and his immobilized, impotent form on the cross. In that outstretched form, we see the full cost of daring to heal. We see not just what healing can lead to, but at its essence, what healing really is: namely, a willingness to take away the sufferings of others even at the cost of bringing them on oneself.

But more than that, in the crucified healer we see how healing can flow from weakness. We are accustomed to seeing healing as a form of power, as action that overrides circumstances and directs outcomes, which we then measure and take to be the mark of success for physicians or hospitals. What the healer on the cross shows us is how healing flows finally from weakness and vulnerability and not from power. Although Christ did use power to heal, in the event of the cross it is not finally power but weakness that heals. The healing weakness of Christ on the cross is a weakness that is freely chosen for the sake of others, a weakness that comes *after power.* It is a recognition of the essential limits of power, not merely the technological limits of our medicine but the inherent limits even of God's power to heal. Power heals but only in a limited or provisional way. For while power—our own or God's—can override circumstances and direct outcomes and thus can truly heal, power overrides or directs only at the risk of negating the selfhood or personhood of the other or at the risk of doing violence to the full circumstances in which the other suffers.

The essence of healing is in the weakness that is after power, and the cross shows us how this weakness can be mightier than power alone in bringing true healing. The weakness that comes after power is truly able to heal not because it gets rid of the pain, but because it is willing to transfer the pain from the one who is sick to the one who heals. Through this willingness to take on the pain of the sufferer, the healer establishes a community with the sufferer that cannot be broken by disease or by pain. Before the cross, Christ the healer is always separate from those in sickness who cry out to him for mercy. On the cross, Christ is one with them and cries out with them and for them. The cry of Christ on the cross is the cry of all who are isolated in suffering, all who are separated by sickness from community, all whose pain separates them from any possibility of community with a God traditionally conceived as all good and all powerful. In that cry, Christ redefines the boundaries of God, placing pain, brokenness, and godforsakenness itself within God, so that those who experience even godforsakeness do so in community with Christ and thus with God.[16] This is the ground upon which Paul can confidently declare that nothing in "all creation, will be able to separate us from the love of God in Christ Jesus our Lord" (Rom. 8:39).

Before the cross, Christ heals by removing sickness and pain. On the cross, Christ brings physical destruction and pain into God and so expands the compass of the triune community of God so that it embraces, in its own experience, destruction and pain. Before the cross, Christ heals what can be healed by power. On the cross, Christ heals what can only be healed in weakness, through the community for which suffering is no obstacle and for which there can be no quarantine or isolation or hell. This is the community of the cross, the community of Christ with the repentant thief.

The cross is not a repudiation of power but an exposure of the limits of its capacity to heal. The limits of power are exposed on the cross by their transcendence in the form of weakness. Through the weakness of the cross, salvation and healing reach their fullness, beyond the limits of healing through power. The cross is the crucifixion of the healer, the one who uses power to heal but who does not stop healing when power fails. When our medicine fails, we often say we can do no more. The cross contradicts us. Weakness has its own power or efficacy, not as a new technique or procedure, but as the invitation to community in which a surprisingly gracious or unexpected transformation may simply occur.[17] The weakness and the foolishness of the cross, as Paul insists, is the power of God that has strength greater than our power (1 Cor. 1:18–25). In this way the cross exposes the danger that we will put power per se ahead of healing, that we will exercise our medical power even when it ceases to heal, or that we will come to believe that power is the only way or the most important way to help others. In the community of the cross, the strong and weak exchange places; the strong are made weak by their oneness with the weak, and the weak heal the strong through the mystery of that grace made perfect in weakness.

This expresses the truth behind Stanley Hauerwas's warning that we use medicine as power to separate ourselves from those in pain. We look to medicine to help us avoid being present with those who suffer. As a technology, medicine controls the relationship between the healthy and the sick, keeping the ill and their suffering from disturbing the well. For instance, in the case of dying children, a "mutual pretense" is often practiced by parents, children, and the medical staff which forbids any discussion of terminal illness. Since the primary means of fighting terminal illness is a series of increasingly intrusive medical technologies, a dying child often grows alienated or estranged from parents or older adults who could offer care and compassion in the child's suffering and death.[18] However, if we learn first to be in the presence of suffering, then medicine has a useful and proper role. Without this qualification, medicine is used as a means to avoid our responsibilities to care for the ill. In that case, "we do not need a community capable of caring for the ill; all we need is an instrumental rationality made powerful by technological sophistication."[19]

According to Hauerwas, we should not look to medicine to insulate us from suffering. To care for the suffering is a moral task, and "the ability to sustain such care in the face of suffering and death is no easy enterprise, for the constant temptation is to try to eliminate suffering through the agency of medicine rather than let medicine be the way we care for each other in our suffering."[20] Suffering alienates us from one another; and medicine can, at least potentially, increase rather than decrease the alienation. For in medicine, the healthy or strong help the weak and suffering, thereby emphasizing their strength at the expense of those who suffer. Hauerwas explains:

> We feel we must be very strong to be able to help the weak and needy. We may be right about that, but we may also fail to understand the kind of help they really need. Too often we seek to do something rather than first simply learn how to be with, to be present to, the sufferer in his or her loneliness.[21]

In this respect, Hauerwas echoes the warning of Paul Ramsey: "The patient has entered a covenant with the physician for his complete *care,* not for continuing useless efforts to *cure.*" Ramsey goes on to add: "If the sting of death is sin, the sting of dying is solitude." Consequently, medicine has created a dilemma where "desertion is more choking than death, and more feared. The chief problem of the dying is how not to die alone." In such situations, "the sound of human voices and the clasp of the hand may be as important in keeping company with the dying as . . . relieving their pain."[22]

The crucifixion of the healer reveals to us that the essence of healing is to be found in the weakness that is after power, the weakness and even the pain we accept for ourselves as the condition for our remaining in community with the sick. But today we have come to believe that pain is to be avoided at all costs and so that power is the only response to the pain of others.

The growing power of our medical technology tempts us to use it to avoid the presence of those who are sick. This danger, however, must not lead us into an even greater temptation: namely, to reject the use of medicine. To act with the aid of medical technologies is not necessarily to succumb to a presumptuous temptation. When we use the power of medicine, we expose ourselves to the risk that it will pervert us into people incapable of participation in the community of the cross. But that risk does not justify renouncing medicine, least of all in the name of the one who died on the cross, for Christ acted in power to heal.

Our challenge is to learn to use medicine, including medical genetics in its prenatal applications, in company with the crucified healer and in the community of the cross, to recognize medicine's powers and its limits, and most of all to learn to use medicine without letting it keep us from healing through our weakness.

How does Jesus Christ as fellow sufferer *and* healer, as the crucified *and* resurrected One, inform our use of a medicine that can both help to ameliorate and inflict suffering? The answer is not simply that good technology stops suffering while bad technology ignores it or increases it. The theological purpose of medical technology is not to manage pain but to allow us to participate in God's redemptive work, which we plainly see in Jesus Christ as a process full of pain and vulnerability.

In the face of this perplexing ambiguity of the cross's redemptive power, James McClendon offers some instructive and suggestive observations on suffering. He insists that creation and suffering cannot be separated; the two are integrally related.[23] Their strong relationship can be seen in mundane forms of creativity that reflect "the idea that creation is intrinsically costly. It has its price. There is no scientific or artistic or political creation, no new state, no work of high art, no product of hard thought but takes it toll upon the artisan."[24] Suffering is both a result and a means of creativity. A creator pays the price of sacrifice, dedicated and disciplined effort, enduring hardship and setbacks as well as risking various responses to his or her creative efforts. The subsequent creation, such as an idea or artifact, may also, whether intentionally or unwittingly, inflict suffering on others, eliciting from them in turn a creative response. To eliminate suffering would also mean removing a principal stimulus to creativity.

The relationship between suffering and creativity is not confined to human creativity but includes natural or evolutionary processes. The creativity and suffering associated with human history is itself rooted in larger natural processes and environments. Humans "are part and parcel of the universe, and live in symbiosis with other living things and in mutual dependence."[25] Hence we are part of "a cosmos of dynamic, open emergence."[26] Human creativity is not pursued in isolation from but within and dependent upon emerging natural options. Human history and cultures can find no clean escape from the defining and limiting characteristics of randomness and chance. Our growing awareness of this contingency, however, exacts a high price, for "the higher into this complex sphere of consciousness and self-consciousness that nature rises, the more evident are the struggle, suffering, and evil that accompany all its creativity."[27] In short, "the rise of consciousness more generally means a new access to pain."[28]

McClendon, like Paul but unlike many modern theologians, assumes that suffering is a given fact of creaturely existence rather than a problem to be overcome or solved. For Christians, the moral task is not to try to explain why a good God allows evil to occur[29] or simply to put a stop to it, but to incorporate suffering into their moral life. Indeed, Christians are called "to share the *excruciating* way of the cross."[30]

As revealed in creation itself and even more clearly in the crucifixion, suffering is intrinsic to the life of the triune God and should be entered into by the church as a dimension of our life in the Spirit. "Creation's suffering . . . is the labor of a woman giving birth, God's labor pains . . . are those of creation . . . and the two, God's and the world's, are mediated, brought together, by the labor pains of the Christian [community], who in company with their Master suffered and were sustained by God who is Spirit."[31]

Pastors who accompany those in pain inevitably suffer themselves. If we provide theological companionship to those undergoing the trauma of prenatal genetic testing, we can expect to find ourselves wounded. Sometimes pastors observe that, in a day's work, they must go from the joy of childbirth to the bedside of the dying. In prenatal genetics, these polar opposites can merge: pregnancy and birth may collide with sickness and death in a single experience. Pastors who are truly present in such a occurrence, who are open to its pain and vulnerable to its grief, will inevitably suffer. More than knowledge and skill are needed. The heart must be strong, for it will surely be bruised.

Genetics, Medicine, and the Cross

What then can we say of the relationship between the cross, which stands at the center of the Christian faith, and the question of selective abortion, which looms at the dimly lit horizon of faith? Is selective abortion ever an option for those who seek either to practice or to use medicine within the community of the cross?

The answers given by contemporary theologians vary widely. Some argue that prenatal human genetics should be limited to diagnostic and therapeutic techniques. Genetic science should help physicians make more accurate diagnoses, develop new therapies, and prescribe therapy with precise accuracy. Genetic science should not be used, they argue, to prevent the birth of persons with genetic conditions. Genetic science and technology may be used to cure sickness, but to use it to test and abort fetuses or to try to improve the gene pool of the human race is an assault upon the dignity of the fetus and the meaning of humanity. Other theologians, as we saw in chapter 1, offer a different view of Christian responsibility in the face of a difficult genetic prediction.

Our purpose here is not to give advice but to invite thought. Rather than argue for one view, we will trace out two lines of thinking that could flow from what we have already explored in this chapter. The meaning of healing, community, pain, and hope is to be found in the cross of Jesus Christ. What does the suffering of the crucified healer mean to those who are undergoing prenatal genetic testing? Can it mean anything to the unborn subject of the tests? How can it guide the actions of those who must decide what to do in light of testing?

One line of thinking might focus on Jesus' compassion for the weak, the children, the most vulnerable, and conclude that all abortion—but especially that for genetic purposes—is inconsistent with this compassionate nature. Further, many will point to the way in which modern medicine isolates the sufferer from the community, removing the one who is sick from the view of others, so that they do not have to face sickness, fragility, and mortality. Selective abortion could easily be seen as the worst possible development of this tendency in modern medicine. Through abortion, the chronically sick and the genetically affected are entirely removed, not just from our communities or from our hospital wards, but from life itself. The same fear that isolates the sick is what drives the selective termination of the genetically affected. In both cases, it is a fear wholly inconsistent with the demands of the gospel to accept the weak and the sick as part of the renewed community. Many Christians are likely to regard such thoughts as amounting to a powerful, even overwhelming, case against selective abortion—perhaps against all abortion.

A second line of thinking will take quite a different view of the relationship between the crucified healer and the process of prenatal genetic testing, including the question of selective abortion. Three points can be noted in this line of thinking.

1. *The status of the fetus as a person.* The fetus at the stage when prenatal screening is performed is simply not yet part of the human community. Although perhaps ethically generous, it is biologically and theologically erroneous to regard a fetus, at the fetal age when testing is done, as a human person. This argument depends, of course, on careful theological analysis of the development of the fetus, a subject that theologians have been largely hesitant to undertake but which we will explore in chapter 7. Here we only want to point out that if the fetus at eighteen weeks' fetal age is not to be regarded as a person, then it would be wrong to see it as a vulnerable person most befriended by Jesus and thus most worthy of protection by Christians.

2. *The limits of scientific power.* While our power in prenatal and genetic medicine is significant, it is far from unlimited. If our power were greater, if in particular we possessed the ability not only to diagnose but to treat, no one would hesitate to recommend treatment as theologically and morally preferable to selective termination. Treatment would be almost everyone's first choice; but when it is not possible, does termination become an acceptable second choice? The fact that we have power to diagnose but not power to treat, that we have a little power but not much, forces us into a new and difficult zone or context. Before technological advances in prenatal genetics, we did not know the health of the fetus. Now we partly know it but can do little to change it. It is precisely because of our limited power—the limited power of our medical technology, our limited power to cope with disease, our limited power to meet all our responsibilities—that we may choose a least-bad outcome. If we had greater power or even greater social support, we might be able to choose otherwise; therefore, our choice may be different under future circumstances. The

choice of abortion may thus be seen not as an arrogant misuse of power but fundamentally as a confession of weakness, of the frustrations we feel at the limits of our capacity to live out other possibilities.

3. *The costs of abortion.* The observation that abortion is costly to those who choose it is often exaggerated and confused in the general debate surrounding abortion. Those arguing against access to abortion point out what they consider to be severe psychological consequences to women who elect an abortion. Our aim here is not to magnify the difficulty of abortion and to make of this an argument against it, but to try to recognize the actual extent of the difficulties attendant upon an abortion, especially one elected for genetic reasons.

The grief of wanting a pregnancy but being unable to accept it for genetic reasons is deep, real, and lasting. Isolation, pain, and guilt are often part of the experience. No one chooses this because it is easy or because it avoids pain. "I have been completely unprepared for the magnitude of the loss, the depth of the wound," writes "Rose Green."[32] Far from isolating the sick (the fetus) from the well (the parents, in particular the mother), the process of genetic testing and selective abortion binds parents (again, especially the mother) and offspring in an intimate community of weakness and pain. In this community of weakness and pain, suffering is common property and might even be seen as transferred from the fetus, who will not live with the pain brought by the genetic condition, to the mother and perhaps to the father, who will continue to bear their pain.

Without any doubt, many will choose to abort a genetically affected fetus for reasons of social pressure or because of an arrogant but flawed hope for perfection in childbearing. However, could it not also be possible that a few will choose to terminate a genetically affected pregnancy because they want so much to remove the pain of this condition from their offspring but, because they are wholly unable to remove the pain, are willing to transfer some portion of it to themselves through the choice of abortion? In this way, could they not be acting in the community of the cross, in communion with the crucified healer?

7

Human Genetics in Light of the Resurrection

Brenda, a pastor on the staff of a large church, received a call from an obstetrician in the congregation.

"I don't know who else to ask," he said. "One of my patients is scheduled for a therapeutic abortion. The genetic tests look pretty bad, so I think they're doing the right thing.

"But they're devout Christians, and their pastor told them what they're doing is a sin. He even said that the fetus has a soul but that there could be no funeral or baptism or anything like that. Apparently he went on and on about resurrection and judgment and all that. They were already pretty upset about it and, well, I'm afraid this will put them over the edge. I'm meeting them in about an hour. Do you think you could join us?"

The resurrection of the crucified healer is the center point of Christian faith. Our previous discussions about creation, redemption, and healing have little meaning unless they are rooted in this core of our faith. And our theological and moral inquiries concerning parental responsibility for the fetus must also be grounded in this core. Without this center point, moral discernment and pastoral care are incomplete and ineffectual.

The resurrection of Jesus Christ shapes the pattern, structure, and content of New Testament literature. Proclamation, exhortation, descriptions, and instruction presuppose and bear witness to the One that God raised from the dead. Each of the Gospels, for instance, ends with an account of the empty tomb or an appearance of the resur-

111

rected Jesus. Paul insists that Christ was "raised to life" and "appeared to Cephas, and afterward to the Twelve" as well as to James and "all the apostles" (1 Cor. 15:4–7).[1]

Paul, however, insists that the resurrected Christ is but "the first-fruits of the harvest of the dead" (1 Cor. 15:20). Drawing upon Jewish apocalyptic imagery,[2] Paul proclaims that "in Christ all will be brought to life" (1 Cor. 15:22). Christ's resurrection is not a bizarre and isolated event consigned to the past but a sign of the eventual destiny of all creation. What happened to Jesus in and following his death, Paul insists, will also occur, in the fullness of time, in the lives and deaths of believers. Indeed, its meaning extends to embrace all of creation.[3]

It must be stressed that Paul is not teaching a doctrine of spiritual immortality or disembodied survival. Paul affirms the belief common to the Judaism of his time that human beings are not composed of two separable parts, body and soul, so that the soul is capable of living eternally without the body. All creatures, including humans, are embodied. The great fear of *Sheol* in the Hebrew Scriptures was the "horror of the 'naked soul.'"[4] And it is one's entire being—soul, mind, and body—that is created, redeemed, and resurrected into the eternal life of God. As John Polkinghorne has observed, "when we come to talk of the hope given to all humankind in Christ, we are not talking about spiritual survival but about resurrection, the reconstruction of the psychosomatic being, even if the new body is a glorified one, as Paul's phrase 'a spiritual body' *(soma pneumatikon)* suggests."[5] For the most part, the focus of Christian hope in the New Testament is resurrection rather than the immortality of the soul.[6] This ancient Christian view of the fundamental oneness of body and soul, so often abandoned by philosophers and theologians alike in later centuries,[7] is now more at home once again in the intellectual world of our age, shaped by neuroscience. "We may view this modern understanding as in line with the intentions of the earliest Christian anthropology [of] the early fathers [who] defended our psychosomatic unity as a basic principle of Christian anthropology."[8]

It was their belief in the resurrection of the body that compelled the early Christian theologians to affirm the importance and value of the body and to investigate its eternal destiny. The theology of the past two centuries, however, has tended to diminish or radically reinterpret the centrality of resurrection for Christian faith. Modern theologians, for the most part, have construed Christ's resurrection in one of two ways. Some emphasize that Christ's resurrection is unique, unrepeatable, and not fully comprehensible,[9] not an event of history as we ordinarily think of that word. "Even theologians, including quite orthodox theologians," according to Macquarrie, "hesitate to say that the resurrection of Jesus was historical in any ordinary sense."[10] Other modern theologians insist that the resurrection has little or nothing to do with Jesus' actual fate following his death but is an episode in the troubled lives of his early followers.[11] As Polkinghorne has observed, "it has been suggested that what happened was a faith event in the minds of the disciples, a conviction achieved after a period of reflection, that the cause of Jesus continued beyond his death."[12]

Early theologians also found difficulty in the concept of resurrection. From the outset, Christian theologians found themselves at odds with views of history and human nature that were current in their surrounding culture, especially the culture shaped by Greek philosophy.[13] And from that culture, many Christians took up the idea of an immortal soul that is separable from the body at death.

Within the last thirty years, however, theologians such as Jürgen Moltmann and Wolfhart Pannenberg have tried to recover resurrection as the central Christian doctrine. Both argue that without a central and vital belief in resurrection, there is no realistic or viable base for Christian hope and eschatology, and that all such hope is grounded in the historicity of Jesus' resurrection. According to Pannenberg, "If Jesus had not been raised from the dead, it would be impossible to ascribe any saving meaning to his death, for that death could then only have meant the failure of his mission and nothing more."[14] Moltmann is equally adamant, insisting that the "Easter witnesses" reflect "objective certainty" in their reports "about the event of the raising of Jesus."[15] Pannenberg insists that the first Easter is the crucial historical episode that sustains Christian faith throughout time: "In the resurrection of Jesus we therefore have to do with the sustaining foundation of Christian faith. If this collapses, so does everything else which the Christian faith acknowledges."[16] Moltmann is insistent, declaring that the "raising by God was experienced by the Christ who 'was crucified, dead, and buried.' It is only in this interrelation that the raising acquires its special saving meaning."[17]

God's raising of Jesus from the dead also marks the hope and eschatological destiny of creation. Since sin and death were conquered in the death of Jesus, then all creatures redeemed by this victory will share in the new life of the resurrected Christ. As Pannenberg explains: "The forgiveness of sins and life in faith, hope, and love through the power of the Holy Spirit are the present dawn of future life in communion with God; and the Christian hope of the resurrection of the body is directed towards this consummation."[18] This hope is both personal and cosmic in its scope, leading Moltmann to claim: "'*The resurrection of the dead*' means human persons. '*The resurrection of the body*' means human nature. Only '*resurrection of nature*' will complete the horizon of expectation that belongs to this hope."[19]

Recent theology is recovering the early Christian emphasis on the resurrection of the body because we are also recovering the awareness that we human beings are psychosomatic unities that are either raised in the wholeness of this unity or not raised at all. We are rejecting the idea that only in humanity is to be found a substance, the soul, that is capable of immortality and for whose immortal bliss the entire nonpsychic creation was made only to be destroyed. We are recognizing that we can only speak coherently of our own resurrection as physical creatures if we can also speak of the resurrection of the whole physical creation. Furthermore, we are finding in the resurrection of the body of Jesus Christ a ground for the hope of the renewal, not just of ourselves as physical beings, but for the renewal of all creation. Jesus Christ is being understood more and more as the cosmic Christ through whom community with God is opened not for disembodied souls but for the entire cosmos.

If we can speak coherently of the resurrection of the body, and if we also can speak of the resurrection of the whole creation, we likewise can struggle to speak coherently of the resurrection of the unborn, the developmentally impaired, the aborted. We do not confer upon them, just as we do not confer upon ourselves, a metaphysical substance of the soul that requires their immortality. Rather, we simply recognize that a God who in Christ makes all things new may in mercy choose to include those who never attain extra-uterine life. For just as the God who raised Jesus Christ will transfigure the physical creation which surrounds us like a womb, so God will also transfigure that physical creation inside the human womb. We cannot escape the conclusion that "the intuition that our destiny is intimately bound up with the destiny of the cosmic womb from which we were born forces one to try to grope for that wider meaning" of the redemption of the whole cosmos.[20] But neither can we avoid the conviction that the microcosmic creation within is included in the biblical declaration that all things will be made new.

We are nature-being-transformed, and we exist in a cosmos undergoing transfiguration. This is our moral context. Oliver O'Donovan insists, quite rightly, "that Christian ethics depends upon the resurrection of Jesus Christ from the dead."[21] Because God raised Christ from the dead, Christians are not saved *from* creation but live in the hope of the redemption *of* creation. Christ's resurrection reveals the purpose of God's creation and redemption of the world in general and human beings in particular. Resurrection establishes a moral order because it is the starting point as well as the end of God's creative and redemptive intentions.

For O'Donovan, the recognition of the resurrection as the moral order for Christian ethics leads to a critical rejection of modern attempts to forge our own destiny, especially through genetics. O'Donovan's uneasiness with medical attempts to alter the shape of human life is directed primarily against its accompanying moral intolerance. Technological interventions into nature in general and into human life in particular are often guided, O'Donovan believes, by simplistic assumptions regarding a normative but malleable structure of life, which can be manipulated through human knowledge and skill. Those who oppose or question these attempts are wrongly judged to be morally deficient and to be standing in the way of progress.

O'Donovan urges us to approach reproductive technology with caution and a tolerance that "comes from taking moral questions so seriously that we recognize the point at which they exceed our competence to resolve them."[22] Much of our modern technological culture not only fails to recognize the limits of human competence, but intentionally and categorically ignores the eschatological intent of God revealed in a resurrected order. We can make proximate moral judgments, "but when it comes to pronouncing a verdict on a human being's life in its totality, we know that too much is hidden from us to permit any anticipation of God's final word."[23] Consequently, our technological interventions reflect a banal satisfaction of our wants and desires more than a longing to conform to the moral order of Christ's resurrection.

It is in the moral order of Christ's resurrection "that the shape of a human life is decisively established."[24] Hence, the principal moral question that must be asked of acts that apply our technical skill is: "What do they count for eternity?" Or more explicitly, how can life in general, and specific moral acts in particular, "belong to the renewed and transformed world which God is bringing into being[?]"[25] O'Donovan answers:

> The issues of morality are as complex and diverse as the created order which gives rise to them are reduced to a stark and awesome simplicity. We can speak of this simple choice for or against God's new creation, the simple alternative of a broad way and a narrow way, the straightforward either–or opposition of sin and virtue.[26]

This "awesome simplicity" is necessary and vital for Christian ethics, "for without it morality loses its eschatological relation to the new creation and becomes no more than a reflection of the ambiguities and complications of this world."[27]

If the resurrection of Christ brings with it the transformation of the entire cosmos, including of ourselves as physical beings, what then of the transformation of the fetus that is diagnosed with a serious genetic or chromosomal disorder? Does the transformation of the cosmos in Christ include the transformation of the microcosmic—

namely, the human fetus that fails to survive or is aborted for genetic reasons? Are they joined with Christ in death, and will they therefore be joined with Christ in resurrection? And if we see the genetically affected fetus as joined with Christ in suffering and death and thus included in the hope of resurrection, how would such a vision inform or shape parental moral decisions regarding the use of genetic and reproductive technology? These are the unavoidable theological questions of the next decade and the next century.

Does the Fetus Have a Soul?

For many people today, the question of eternal life is nothing other than the question of an immortal soul. If we ask, "Is the aborted fetus immortal?" we are thought really to be asking whether it possesses an immortal soul. Likewise, to say that at conception the preembryo is a human person with a soul is to say that the preembryo is a person who will have eternal life.

We see many problems with this approach, not the least of which is that it is contradicted by the biblical writers' most characteristic view of humanity. They did not see "the soul" as a thing to be possessed or as a metaphysically separable substance blessed with an intrinsic immortality capable of surviving the body. Instead, they viewed the human person as body-with-soul, a psychosomatic unity, which wholly dies at death and for whom the only hope of immortality lies in the resurrection of the body-with-soul in the general resurrection at the end of history.

Nevertheless, the language of the soul arises so often in discussions about the fetus that we must consider its claims as well as its difficulties. Those who refer to "the soul" may be religious believers who think they are correctly using the language of their religious tradition. Or they may be secular writers drawing on a Western philosophical tradition, perhaps seeking to reconcile that tradition with contemporary neuroscience and embryology. Of course, the pedigrees of ideas cannot be disentangled neatly, for theological and philosophical ideas have been indiscriminately mixed over the millennia. Modern notions of "person," for example, have come to psychology and to popular culture from theology, where it first meant "relation" within the unity of the triune God:

> Trinitarian discussion of the term also had an anthropological impact as "person" came to denote what was specific to Father, Son, and Spirit in their mutual relations. If the personhood of Jesus is that of the eternal Son in relation to the Father, all individuals are persons in virtue of the relation to God, which is the basis of their whole existence. [28]

This theological source, of course, is long forgotten in modern culture, and so now a person is understood to exist in social relation with other human persons but not, as originally and properly understood, also in relation to the three persons of the Trinity.

Embryology itself is not a purely scientific or philosophical inquiry, but has been pursued, from its outset in the West, in interaction with theological themes. In the first five centuries of the Christian era, ideas about embryology were involved in at least three major areas of doctrinal debate. In the early fourth century, for instance, the Arian controversy drew attention to the meaning of the relationship of Christ as "the only begotten Son of the Father." Theologians at the Council of Nicea and in the ensuing decades struggled to specify the differences between divine and human begetting as part of their effort to develop the doctrine of the Trinity.

In the early fifth century, Augustine drew upon theories of conception to try to understand original sin. How could it be that Adam and Eve had brought on themselves a condition of disorder that could be passed on biologically to their offspring? Finally, in the Christological controversy of the mid-fifth century, which wrestled with the question of the unity of the human and divine natures in Christ, theologians considered how the conception and birth of Jesus of Nazareth should be understood in light of the doctrine that Jesus Christ is the second person of the Trinity incarnate. Various embryological theories were available to the theologians who participated in these debates, and sometimes theologians debated over competing versions of embryology. For instance, sixteenth-century Protestant theologians appealed to competing theories of human conception in their debates over the nature of the humanity that Christ assumed in the incarnation.[29]

For embryology to play a role in theology is nothing new. What is new is that embryology is no longer just a science but also a technology, and theological interpretations of embryology will play a determinative role in the use of this technology. Today the issue is not merely what will we *think* about the embryo and the developing fetus, but what will we *do* with embryos and how will we intervene in the development of the fetus. It is no longer sufficient to ask the relatively safe question of how science affects our theology; we must now ask how our theology will determine the use of our technology.

The early theological debates on Christology or the doctrine of the Trinity are likely to give way in the twenty-first century to debate on the manipulation of the embryo and the fetus.[30] This theological debate will be resolved not in a council but in the clinic, not by elderly clergy but by young women and couples, and not in ecclesiastical but by economic structures. For this challenge the church today needs not just a theological anthropology but a *theological embryology*. How are we to understand the humanity and the personhood of the fetus? How should our theological understanding of the fetus be informed by scientific understandings of the details of fetal development, for instance, the in utero development of a neural system?

One approach, of course, is to understand the true core of the human person as the soul, metaphysically distinct from the body and probably capable of immortality apart from the body. The history of Western thought about the soul is complex, but those who see it as a metaphysically distinct substance typically understand it to be a substance different from the physical matter that composes the body and the brain. An alternative approach is to see the human "soul" as extraordinary mental, emotional, and spiritual powers of the human person, but as existing in the complexity of the physical stuff of which our bodies are made and not in a different substance. Seen this way, the soul or the personal life of the human individual ceases to function when the body and brain cease to function, and so must be considered dead. The person or soul is not intrinsically capable of immortality and will live after this life only if the body is resurrected and with it the capacity for personal consciousness is restored.

Philosophers and theologians on both sides of the argument have tried to link their concept of the soul to speculations about fetal development and occasionally to the observations of experimental embryology. Thinkers influenced by Aristotle, for instance, believed that the individual human soul gives form to the physical matter of the body and thus is present in the fetus only when the form of the human body is visible, at least several weeks after the beginning of fetal development. Much later, as the role of genetic material was beginning to be understood, the argument was made that since the genetic material provides the form of the body, and since it is all there at conception, the soul must be present at conception.[31]

Today, the use of embryology as a source for our theological and philosophical understanding of the fetus has sparked a new debate. A central issue is what light the science of fetal development can shed on the question of the presence of the individual human soul or human personhood in the developing fetus. Can science play a role in helping to indicate when personhood is present? Some have argued, for instance, for a concept of "brain life" comparable to the definition of "brain death" that has been introduced into medicine in recent decades. If brain death at the end of life can be defined as a measurable neurological state, is it consistent—perhaps even required for the sake of consistency—that we define brain life at the beginning of individual existence in a way that is measurable, perhaps by reference to the development in the fetus of specific anatomical structures of the brain?[32]

It may seem appealingly simple to be able to point to specific anatomical structures exhibited in the neuromaturation of the fetus and to be able to conclude, with objectivity, that "brain life" has been achieved and thus that consciousness or personhood is present. But it is philosophically dubious to argue from the presence of a physical structure such as the neocortex to the conclusion that a *metaphysical reality* such as *personhood* is also present. Mario Moussa and Thomas A. Shannon point out the obvious difficulty: "Perhaps the most striking aspect of neuromaturation, at least from the standpoint of our argument, is that the central nervous system is among the first systems to begin and probably the last to complete development. Many neurobiologists argue that the reticulo-cerebral complex continues to develop even into preadolescence."[33] This process of neurological development has no dramatic moments when obvious metaphysical milestones (such as the transition to personhood) are attained. Therefore how can we on strictly scientific grounds specify the point in the process when personhood is present?

Our efforts to think about the personhood of the fetus in light of embryology are complicated further when we consider the wide range of ways in which fetal development can be impaired by chromosomal or genetic abnormalities. A severely impaired fetus (such as an anencephalic) will never develop the minimal neurological prerequisites of a mental life. Such a fetus will fail nearly any neuromaturation test for personhood. But aside from such severe impairments, the ability of genetically affected fetuses to attain the neurological conditions for personhood will depend on how personhood is defined in relationship to the neurological. We are thus brought back to the same problem: namely, on what grounds can we determine the stage of neuromaturation at which personhood is present?

Answering this question is not merely technically difficult, as if more research in embryology would bring us closer to an answer. "Personhood cannot be discovered biologically, as it is a social and moral construct."[34] The science of fetal development will not reveal the minimal biological conditions of personhood. However, in the future, our science will reach a clearer understanding of the role that genes play in fetal development and of how abnormal genetic or chromosomal patterns impair that development. At that time, we will probably find ourselves tempted to define scientifically when a fetus becomes a person, which fetus attains personhood at which point, and which one is impaired in reaching personhood, perhaps forever.

It is altogether appropriate for us to try to understand the relationship between fetal development, including impaired development, and the attainment of personhood. But we should not expect that scientific research itself will give an answer, as if the answer to our metaphysical question is there in the physics, the *physis,* the nature of the thing. Personhood is a metaphysical and theological concept. Ideally it is informed by, and can be expressed in, embryological terms; but it is not reducible to them. For example, personhood may require the development of the rudiments of the central nervous system, but it is not synonymous with the existence of this system. "The presence of a single biological entity is the physical precondition for the presence of a person; a functioning nervous system is a presupposition for physical activity; an integrated nervous system is required for intellectual activity. But these biological realities neither guarantee the presence of nor constitute the definition of a person."[35] What we mean by the theological and metaphysical category, "human person," should be consistent with the best insight into fetal development and neuromaturation, and we should be able to express our definition in terms of objectively identifiable biological criteria. Biology will not give us our metaphysics or our theology, but our theology should be expressible in biological terms.

One of the problems faced by anyone attempting an embryological and neurological definition of personhood is an inevitable conflict between the dynamic nature of personhood and the static character of minimal criteria for its attainment. Shortly after the Supreme Court decision in *Roe v. Wade,* Albert Outler offered this definition: "'personhood' is a divine intention operating in a life-long process that runs from nidification till death. It is never perfectly achieved and it is all too often thwarted in ways too tragic for glib rationalizations or even bitter tears. Our personhood is our identity, and this is always experienced as prevenient."[36]

This sense of prevenience captures nicely the dilemma that we face in trying to say which fetus is a person, and when. Except for the most profoundly impaired, each fetus is a prevenient person, not in attainment but in promise, in expectation. In this sense, writers such as Barbara Katz Rothman point out that women who decide to terminate a pregnancy for genetic reasons typically regard the fetus as a baby, not of course as a baby that can be taken home and expected to grow into early childhood. But they view it as a prevenient baby, one who exists in becoming and is loved, wanted, and hoped for; as that which actually exists now in anticipation of what it may become, or might have become, were it not for a specific genetic limitation.

A properly theological understanding of human personhood is founded on what we take to be the destiny of human life in reference to God:

> The human destiny for [community] with God, which finds defini-
> tive realization in the incarnation of the Son, means that humanity
> as such, and each individual within it, is lifted above the natural
> world and even also above the social relations in which we exist.
> The destiny of [community] with God confers inviolability on hu-
> man life in the person of each individual.[37]

This destiny is the ground and the guarantee of the dignity of each individual human person, and thus we possess a dignity that is truly inalienable. "A feature of the dignity that accrues to us by virtue of our being destined for [community] with God is that no actual humiliation that might befall us can extinguish it."[38] For Pannenberg, the image of God is our capacity for community with God.[39]

We are always on our way toward this destiny. Our personhood is not a property we possess; nor is it the result of our having crossed a specifiable threshold in our neuromaturation. It is always incomplete for us in this life, but the dignity of our humanity is not undermined by our incompleteness as persons. In this regard, Pannenberg suggests a helpful distinction between personhood and selfhood: Personhood as a concept must include this sense of incompleteness, of prevenience, of destiny, while selfhood refers to the dignity of the self that we are at each stage of this journey toward personhood. For Pannenberg, selfhood is "identity in all individual life. This is true even over a stretch of time, hence selfhood never achieves definitive manifestation in life. It does not yet appear who we truly are, but we exist now as persons."[40] "In the person, then, the integration of the individual moments of life results in an identity of authentic selfhood."[41]

But what are we to make, then, of the one whose life ends at the earliest moments? How are we to understand the personhood of the preembryo that fails to implant or that, after being conceived in vitro, is discarded? How are we to understand our social relationship and our moral obligations to the one whose development is impaired to the point that theological destiny for community with God seems wholly impossible because a genetic destiny has intervened?

Resurrection of the Impaired and the Incomplete

In Augustine's long inquiry in *The City of God* into the end of history and the resurrection of the dead, he speculated that resurrected bodies would contain "no deformity, no infirmity, no languor, no corruption."[42] The general resurrection will mark a comprehensive healing that will "remove and abolish all deformities of the human body, whether common ones or rare and monstrous,"[43] resulting in a condition where "no infirmity shall remain in the mind or body."[44] Unlike a mortal body, a spiritual body will be characterized by its perfect health, beauty, and symmetry. The only exception will be the wounds or scars of martyrs, for these will be worn as "a mark of honor" or "virtue blemishes."[45] Furthermore, one's age at the time of death will have no bearing on the condition or characteristics of one's resurrected body. All, including infants and the aged, "shall rise neither beyond nor under youth, but in that vigor and age to which we know that Christ arrived. For even the world's wisest men have fixed the bloom of youth at about the age of thirty . . . the measure of the age of the fullness of Christ."[46]

Many of Augustine's contemporaries insisted that resurrection was an incredible and irrational belief. How, some scoffed, could amputated limbs that had been destroyed or the bodies of persons eaten by cannibals be restored? Augustine's reply was to ask how such considerations could pose any real challenge to "the Creator" who "created all things out of nothing."[47] Augustine, however, refused to speculate on the eternal fate of aborted fetuses. He is not able "to affirm nor to deny" if they who "were alive in the womb, did also die there, shall rise again."[48]

For Augustine, all human beings, including infants, possess a potentiality that we today would interpret as carried in our genes. This inherent potentiality, for Augustine, comes to expression over time and finally to fulfillment at the end of time: "There is thus, it seems, a kind of pattern already imposed potentially on the material substance of the individual, set out, one might say, like the pattern on a loom; and thus what does not yet exist, or rather what is there but hidden, will come into being, or rather will appear, in the course of time."[49] Here Augustine seems to imagine something like DNA as a kind of hidden, internal information that is reexpressed in its full potentiality in the resurrection. Augustine probably understood this inherent pattern as perfect and thought that human deformities and illnesses were wholly the result of environmental factors, such as injury or poor nutrition. He viewed God as having the power to remove the effects of these assaults to our development and thus to set free the original pattern so that it could be fully complete. As human artists can remove blemishes, so God in resurrection removes the scars and impairments we acquire through living. "Can he not remove all the deformities of the human body, not only the familiar ones but also the rare and the monstrous, such as are in keeping with miseries of this life, but are utterly incongruous with the future felicity of the saints?"[50]

The destiny of those who die before birth perplexed not only Augustine but Gregory of Nyssa as well:

> What wisdom, then, can we trace in the following? A human being enters on the scene of life, draws in the air, beginning the process of living with a cry of pain, pays the tribute of a tear to Nature, just states life's sorrows, before any of its sweets have been his, before his feelings have gained any strength; still loose in all his joints, tender, pulpy, unset; in a word, before he is even human (if the gift of reason is man's peculiarity, and he has never had it in him), such an one, with no advantage over the embryo in the womb except that he has seen the air, so short-lived, dies and goes to pieces again; being either exposed or suffocated, or else of his own accord ceasing to live from weakness. What are we to think about him? How are we to feel about such deaths?[51]

Gregory's apprehensiveness is echoed in our own century by Austin Farrer, who asks:

> We do not know how we should relate to the mercy of God beings who never enjoy a glimmer of reason. Are they capable of eternal salvation or not? . . . The baby smiled before it died. Will God bestow immortality on a smile? Shall we say that every human birth, however imperfect, is the germ of personality, and that God will give it an eternal future? We shall still have to ask why the fact of being born should be allowed a decisive importance; we shall wonder what of children dying in the womb or suffering abortion; and we shall be at a loss where to draw the line.[52]

But then we must wonder whether the one who dies before birth is fundamentally different from the rest of us who die before we truly complete our lives or fulfill our full potential. "We shall all die with our lives to a greater or lesser extent incomplete, unfulfilled, unhealed."[53] The question of the eternal destiny of the fetus whose development is impaired by its genes and who is aborted is essentially no different from the question of the destiny of every human life.

Indeed, it is the inescapable incompleteness of every human life that truly defines our nature. If we believe we have achieved completeness and fulfillment, it is because we have settled for less than we truly are created to be. "Basic to the personality of each individual is the destiny of [community] with God."[54] The deep sense that we are made for more than this life characterizes Christian thought in every age. At its best, such a longing is not a rejection or negation of the physical but a yearning for the fulfillment of physicality, of bodiliness, in the resurrection, which will not destroy but will transform the physical creation, including human bodies, so that they are capable of eternal community with God.

To picture this transformation, Christian writers through the centuries have appealed to genetics as a metaphor. Paul portrays the transformation from mortality to immortality as the planting and subsequent growth of a seed (1 Cor. 15:35–38).[55] In John's Gospel (12:24–25), a similar saying is attributed to Jesus: Being willing to die and be planted like a seed is the precondition for entrance into eternal community. Gregory of Nyssa routinely used the metaphor of the planted seed to explain and defend the resurrection. Paul's metaphor for the resurrected Christ as the firstborn or the firstfruits is echoed by John Polkinghorne: "The resurrection is the beginning of God's great act of redemptive transformation, the seed from which the new creation begins to grow (cf. 2 Cor. 5:17)."[56] It is as if the ancient writers envisioned the resurrection as a genetic transformation from a mortal plant or animal to an immortal organism.

The hope of individual immortality is really the hope "to be part of a complete creation."[57] The early writers do not expect a spiritual metamorphosis disconnected from nature, but rather a reshaping and renewal of nature into a new creation. This is why we do not hope exclusively for the salvation or survival of souls but anticipate, as the firstfruits of the Spirit, a "harvest of dead men and women resurrected."[58] This transformation is accomplished by the power of God while we are most impotent, that is, while we are dead. In that respect, there is an important difference between the sprouting seed and the process of death, transfiguration, and resurrection. At least as we understand it today, the seed does not die but passes through dormancy; then, of its intrinsic genetic capabilities, it germinates in interaction with its environment, and a new plant—genetically continuous with its predecessor and with the seed—begins to grow. In the resurrection, however, there is both continuity and transformation. Genetics as a metaphor points primarily to continuity, not to transformation, unless of course we assume that in the transformation the genetic structure is itself transformed. We simply do not know how the resurrection will transfigure or transform this creation, making it new. As Paul reminds us, our present knowledge is only partial (cf. 1 Cor. 13:12).

Christian hope is rooted in God's ultimate redemption of creation. The breadth of this eschatological vision is reflected in Paul's imagery:

> I consider that the sufferings of this present time are not worth comparing with the glory about to be revealed to us. For the creation waits with eager longing for the revealing of the children of God; for the creation was subjected to futility, not of its own will but by the will of the one who subjected it, in hope that the creation

itself will be set free from its bondage to decay and will obtain the
freedom of the glory of the children of God. We know that the
whole creation has been groaning in labor pains until now; and not
only the creation, but we ourselves, who have the firstfruits of the
Spirit, groan inwardly while we wait for adoption, the redemption
of our bodies. (Rom. 8:18–23)

The sufferings of the present creation are incommensurate with the
glory of the transfigured creation.

The redemption of creation is nothing less than the "cosmic out-
working of salvation."[59] Here there is no line arbitrarily separating
the redemption of history from nature. A redeemed order involves a
process of transforming all that God has created into a new creation.
It is a cosmic healing that relieves both the suffering of persons and
all creation, because "God will no more abandon the universe than he
will abandon us."[60] Although the ways in which nature and history
are redeemed may differ, they remain joined and inseparable. In
Christ, there is true *ecumenical* salvation, involving the redemption
of the whole created order.

Particularly at a time when we now possess the ability to intervene in the molecular basis of life, it is dangerous to maintain an artificial dichotomy between nature and history. Our historic actions in
nature transform the nature that God is also transforming. The question is simple but inevitable: Do our actions, our transformations,
conform to and cooperate with God's, or do they contradict God's
purposes in the redemption of nature?

The new creation is the present creation in its transfiguration.
"The first creation was *ex nihilo* while the new creation will be *ex vet-
ere*"; that is, it will be brought about by the power of God out of the
existing creation. Our hope is that "the new creation is the divine redemption of the old."[61] Our moral task is to participate in this transformation. This task permits and even requires that we make deliberate, limited, and responsible human interventions into selected
natural processes. It is not theologically sufficient to say that the God
who raised Jesus Christ is transfiguring the entire creation. We must
ask how God's transforming action defines the moral context of our
technological action. Recent theology has begun to consider human

technological impact on the planet, in light of eschatological hopes and apocalyptic fears. Our task here is to inquire about the theological meaning, in light of the hope of the resurrection of the body, about technological actions that affect the body, particularly through prenatal genetics.

Resurrection is the supreme emblem of hope because creation's suffering is buried and raised with Christ into the life of the triune God. Suffering does not remain an inexplicable or cruel fate, for it is redeemed by a God who knows the suffering of a beloved creation. We live in an expectant hope that we will share Christ's destiny. As Polkinghorne has observed: "The resurrection of Jesus is the beginning within history of a process whose fulfillment lies beyond history, in which the destiny of humanity and the destiny of the universe are together to find their fulfillment in a liberation from decay and futility."[62]

Resurrection is also the supreme emblem of hope because it reminds us that suffering will end. Our destiny is community with God, not endless pain. Genuine hopelessness or despair is rooted in a belief that suffering will never end.[63] In practical terms, our hope in resurrection gives us the spiritual strength to endure suffering, because it is not a problem to be avoided but part of creation's labor pains that God is drawing into a transformed newness. Our suffering has meaning because it is known, redeemed, and raised into God's eternal life.

If resurrection is the center point of Christian thinking and acting, then how we think and act toward the genetically affected fetus must be grounded in this center. How are we to understand the meaning of the existence of these fetuses? Do they have a destiny of community with God? Will they participate in the resurrection? How will their existence figure into our own resurrected life?

It hardly needs to be said that Christian theology of the resurrection has no clear answers to such questions. The point is not to fabricate a false clarity about what is almost wholly hidden from us, but simply to insist that our failure to ask the question of *ultimate context*—that is, of eternal destiny—is to fail to locate our lives in their full and proper framework of meaning. Who we are as human beings, as pastors, or as expectant parents, is ultimately defined in reference to the destiny for which God has created us. And who or what the genetically affected fetus is, and whether it is best loved by termination or not, must be understood in the same frame of reference.

Any decision is a fork in the road of the story of our lives. It is the choice of one path over others. When we are forced to make any difficult decision, we find ourselves grieving for the other roads that might have been taken but are now lost to us forever. The pathway we choose, the relationships we form, and the life that we build comprise the life that will, in some way unknown to us, be transformed so that it may be alive forever with the transfigured creation in the community of God.

At the very least, a decision about what to do with a genetically affected fetus should be seen as a momentous decision that fundamentally defines the persons we will be, now and forevermore. The report of a prenatal genetic test is a fork in the road—one from which there is no retreat, no avoidance, and for which there is no moral signpost. The choice we take defines who we are now and thus who we will be in the resurrection. For regardless of our decision, we will be raised as the person who was forced to make it and who actually chose one path or another. If our choice is truly to be grounded in Christian faith and hope, it must be made in reference to the person that we believe we are becoming by the transforming power of God that is already at work in our lives. Every choice is a response to this transforming grace. The most relevant consideration in every difficult decision is the extent to which each choice may close us off or open us more expectantly toward this transforming grace.

But we must also ask about the fetus as a distinct entity in the resurrection. Apart from the fact that our lives are changed forever by the event of a difficult pregnancy, does the fetus itself have a place in the resurrection? We do not believe that embryos that fail to implant or that fetuses that abort spontaneously or are aborted, for whatever reason, will be raised as the full persons they might have become, as if they possessed within them an essential nature or soul whose development was thwarted, whether for natural or technological reasons. None of us possesses such an essential nature. Our "soul," or the core of our personhood, is the result of our having lived, the result of relationships, choices, and environmental interactions. The identity of this self or soul is wholly contingent upon the choices and circumstances of our life. At each moment in our past, we could have become other than we are; and at each moment in our future, the identity of our lives remains to be established.

When we hope for resurrection, we hope for this identity-in-development to be continued, as it were, under circumstances wholly mysterious to us now, but with enough continuity so that we will remember then who we are now and live then as the persons that we have become now. This is almost entirely meaningless and impossible when we apply it to the fetus, much less to the embryo or to the preembryo that is not implanted. They do possess genetic identity and (at least after the possibility of twinning) genetic individuality, so we might even say they possess an individual human identity which should be accorded great respect. But they have not yet entered into personhood. As part of the physical cosmos that God creates, they will be included in the transfiguration of all things and exist in the transformed or redeemed cosmos. They cannot be included as human persons but only as a part of the physical creation that was on its way toward personhood. They will not exist then as subjects that regret their circumstances in this life or that blame us or God for their genetic condition or for the brevity of their life.

This is not to say that we will not regret their genetic condition, the painful brevity of their lifespan, or the traumatic choices that their condition thrust upon us. The end of their life is the end of our life with them. Just as they are cut off from being persons at all, so we are cut off from becoming the persons we would have been with them. This is an occasion of the most profound grief, different and in some ways sharper than the grief we experience at the death of a parent or a friend, for in losing a pregnancy we lose a part of our own future, in this world and the next.

8

The Vocation of Prenatal Parenting

Roger had been in a new pastorate for only a year when he suddenly realized that almost all of the pregnancies that had occurred since his arrival seemed to have one thing in common: Some sort of prenatal screening or testing had been advised. As he mulled this over, he also realized that, while he certainly had tried to be present in offering pastoral care, he had not focused on the testing as an important dimension of the pregnancies.

One Sunday, Roger included an unusual petition in the pastoral prayer: "Be especially near, O holy Creator, to all who nurture human life within; strengthen them especially if they undergo prenatal testing of the health of the life they carry, that they may live and act with a constant awareness of your gracious presence."

After the service, one of the new mothers in the congregation stopped to thank Roger for his prayer. "I didn't know that you knew about this sort of thing."

The next evening, during a meeting of the committee responsible for adult education programs, Roger made an unexpected suggestion, "I think we should offer at least a session, maybe even a short course, on what it means today to become a parent. A lot of couples are faced with whether or not to undergo some sort of prenatal genetic test. Maybe we could have a geneticist or a genetic counselor visit the class."

Choosing whether or not to abort a fetus diagnosed with a severe genetic disorder is a difficult moral decision, largely because it forces us to reconsider basic beliefs about parenting, procreation, health, sex, God, death, and life. In particular, Christians facing the process of prenatal genetic testing are driven to reconsider core theological themes, such as the cross and the resurrection of Jesus Christ, and what these disclose to us about the presence of God, the nature of healing, and the hope of transformation.

It is quite likely that many devout Christians will undergo the process of prenatal genetic testing without considering how their beliefs come to bear on their moral decisions. It is also likely that many sincere clergy will not recognize the relevance of Christian theology for the experience of prenatal testing. Their lack of recognition is a failure to acknowledge that at the center of our Christian faith we worship and serve One who fully shares our human genetic nature, who acts again and again to relieve those who suffer from disease, who is broken in crucifixion, and who rises in a transformed bodily nature and promises such transformation to us. It is also a failure to acknowledge that Christian faith is deeply biological, deeply genetic, and thoroughly incarnational. Because they fail to recognize these truths, many pastors and prospective parents will think that the moral context of their decision is no bigger than the physician's office or the diagnostic center, when in fact the true moral context of their decision comprises the cross and resurrection of Jesus Christ. The overwhelming complexity reduces to a stark simplicity: We are God's, and our lives are being transformed by the redemptive power of the God who raised Jesus from the dead.

This is the "simplicity of decision" of which Oliver O'Donovan speaks. For O'Donovan, the "final question" regarding our lives, our actions, and our character is whether they "belong to the renewed and transformed world which God is bringing into being, and that question can be answered only in terms of the relation to Christ in whom the transformed world is already present to us."[1] Hence, a parental response to a fetus diagnosed with a severe genetic disorder is also a response to Jesus Christ, the crucified healer and the resurrected sufferer.

How can pastors assist parents who must respond to a fetus diagnosed with a severe genetic disorder and help them arrive at this clarity of vision and this simplicity of decision? This simplicity of which we speak is not a naive simplicity that refuses to consider the complexity, to face the difficulties, or to recognize the ambiguities. It is rather the ability to sort through this staggering complexity and unresolvable ambiguity to that which is finally clear and simple. An observation by Oliver Wendell Holmes is instructive: "I do not give a fig for the simplicity this side of complexity, but I would give my life for the simplicity on the other side of complexity."[2] Pastoral care and theological companionship should aim at helping parents arrive at the other side of complexity, equally resisting the temptation to remain on this side of complexity, to become stuck somewhere in the details, or to find false confidence in premature moralizing.

To provide theological companionship is not to urge a specific course of action or to recommend a theological interpretation. It is to be willing to explore theological dimensions, to connect immediate human experience with the foundational themes of the faith, and to walk together across the tenuous bridges of meaning that link our sufferings with those of Jesus Christ on the cross, our efforts to heal with those of the healing Savior, and our hopes with Christ's resurrection.

We do not believe that Christian faith and ethics provide a set of guidelines as to when abortion for genetic reasons is acceptable and when it is not. We agree with Albert Outler that "an undeniable case for some kinds of 'therapeutic' abortions"[3] exists, but we are also convinced that it is now the special duty of Christians to resist the altogether too-easy case made by many in modern secular culture for the abortion of anything that deviates from our dubious standards of acceptability.

To be a Christian parent today, especially in the context of prenatal testing, requires that we resist certain tendencies in our culture as alien to the kind of lives we are called to live. Likewise it means that we affirm a way of life, in regard to healing, pain, and hope, that is grounded in the central themes of our faith. Pastors, we believe, have an obligation to those who would be parents today to call them to accept the vocation of Christian parenting, especially prenatal parenting, and thus to enter into a community of resistance and of affirmation.

A Call to Resistance

Christian communities, in particular expectant parents and their pastors, should resist the tendencies described in the paragraphs that follow, as contradictory to our call to be followers of Jesus Christ.

1. *Routineness of prenatal genetic testing.* As testing becomes more routine, the pressure to test will likely increase. The likelihood that we will come to accept prenatal testing automatically, without so much as a moral pause, should concern us. Elizabeth Kristol has claimed that "pressures to undergo testing are invariably followed by subtle pressures to abort in the event of a positive diagnosis."[4] Or Agnus Clarke has observed that "an offer of prenatal diagnosis implies a recommendation to accept that offer, which in turn entails a tacit recommendation to terminate a pregnancy if it is found to show any abnormality."[5] What should be resisted is the pressure to go along, without personal moral responsibility for the process or for the decisions, as if the decisions had already been made and one should simply cooperate with what is expected.

2. *Viewing procreation as a production process.* Prenatal genetics is creating a culture in which human procreation is giving way to human reproduction, and our sense that we are partners with God in the mysterious event of creation is giving way to the consciousness that we are in partnership with a laboratory in a managed event of production, complete with quality control. There will very likely be a growing demand among expectant parents for physicians to give them perfect babies and even to be liable for defects. Will physicians and laboratories be vulnerable to product liability lawsuits if they fail to deliver a genetically "perfect" baby? Are we turning human beings into commodities that can be designed, ordered, and delivered on schedule?

The ultimate fear, of course, is that we will have become so successful in turning procreation into a managed production process that we will no longer give birth to human beings. Can a product be a person? We must resist the tendency to exert so much prenatal control over the identity of our children that they will be unable to distance themselves appropriately from us and become their own selves.

3. *Replaceability of the fetus.* Closely related to the tendency to view the fetus as a commodity is the cultural tendency to view it as replaceable. If a prenatal genetic test indicates a problem, many will try to console distressed parents with the comment that they can "try again." Although intended to be helpful, the comment assumes that what is lost in the termination of one pregnancy can be replaced by another, as if a car had been stolen and could be replaced by another of equal value. Such an attitude will contribute to the commodification of human life. It fails to recognize the uniqueness of each pregnancy, with its distinct problems and hopes. It circumvents an appropriate grieving for the deep loss of a particular pregnancy.

4. *Potential misuse of behavior genetics.* We are very likely to witness a growing tendency for parents to want to use the findings of behavior genetics to try to determine the behavioral tendencies of their offspring. Recent research on a genetic basis for male homosexuality,[6] for instance, is likely to be the basis for parents requesting prenatal genetic testing so as to eliminate any chance of a "gay" fetus. Such a request must be challenged on scientific grounds, and doubtless it will. But more fundamentally, it needs to be challenged on theological grounds as inconsistent with a gospel of grace.

5. *Inferring a false sense of security.* The growth of prenatal testing is likely to bring with it a feeling that pregnancy and parenting can be risk free, as if a genetic "clean bill of health" were a prediction of a problem-free childhood. Genetic testing is often justified because of "the reassurance it almost always brings."[7] Consequently, a growing reliance on prenatal testing can also create a false sense of assurance. As Elizabeth Kristol has observes:

> Displaced anxiety can lead to artificial peace of mind. In the current climate of testing it is all too easy for prospective parents to forget that illness can befall a baby at any time during pregnancy and delivery, or after birth, and that the majority of birth defects are undetectable and unpreventable. Yet, as obstetricians will be the first to admit, many women who receive a negative result on a pre-

natal test seem to feel they are in the clear. This false sense of security can make an undiagnosed birth defect or subsequent illness all the more difficult to handle.[8]

The tendency to resist is to view a genetic test as a broad prediction about the health or even the social well-being of a child which takes the uncertainty and risk out of parenting.

6. *Limiting parental love.* The expansion of prenatal genetic testing may also lead to an increase in the conditional nature of parental acceptance. As Barbara Katz Rothman has observed: "Screening for defects is a way of saying: 'These are my standards. If you meet these standards of acceptability, then you are mine and I will love and accept you totally. After you pass this test'."[9] Unconditional parental love is replaced by a conditional consent based on factors beyond the control of the child. This is incompatible with a Christian understanding of love as agape.

7. *Reinforcing bias against persons with disabilities.* There is growing fear that the use of prenatal genetic testing will encourage social intolerance of those among us with genetic conditions or with other forms of disability. This can occur both in the family and also in the public arena.

In the family, an older sibling with a genetic condition who learns that her mother is undergoing a prenatal genetic test, primarily to test for the recurrence of the same genetic condition, will undoubtedly understand that test as a fundamental assault upon her condition and thus upon her life itself. How can she not conclude, with devastating psychological consequences, that her parents would have prevented her birth and that they must resent her existence?

In the public arena, how can those with disabilities and with genetic conditions not see the widespread increase in testing as our society's desire to rid itself of the presence of all but the "normal"? How can they not fear a growing tide of intolerance and resentment over the cost of their disabilities?[10]

Of all the tendencies that Christians should resist, this may be the most difficult. For while we want to say that we are distinguishing between the person and the condition and affirming the person while trying to prevent the condition, we know that the only way to prevent the condition is to prevent the birth of a person with the condition. If there is any answer, it will lie primarily in action and not in analysis. Will it be possible, whether in the family or in society at large, for us to be a community that uses abortion to prevent the birth of those with certain genetic conditions and, at the same time, is unequivocal in our acceptance of those among us with these same conditions?

8. *Avoidance of pain.* Increased use of prenatal genetic testing seems to fit within a larger popular tendency to avoid pain at all costs. We seek not only pain-free dentistry but a pain-free life. We do not know nor do we want to learn how to make painful experiences part of the narrative of our lives. We shrink from those in pain, fearing that their pain will infect our lives. Is prenatal genetic testing just another way to shrink from the pain of others, in this case by preventing them from living with us? If that is all that prenatal testing is, then it should be resisted as incompatible with the meaning of Christian life in the community of the cross. The goal of the Christian life is not the avoidance of pain but the faithful following of One who enters into the pain of those who suffer.

9. *Managing financial risks.* Prenatal genetic testing is likely to fit within the broader social need to manage health care costs. Regardless of how we fund health care, costs will be more carefully managed in the future. Caring for a person with a genetic condition can be quite expensive. Insurance providers, whether private or public, will have an obvious incentive to manage costs by preventing the birth of genetically affected individuals. They will doubtless see the financial benefit of encouraging parents, perhaps quite strongly, to prevent the birth of children with genetic conditions. How far should this be permitted? Does it represent an illegitimate financial intrusion into a sphere of privacy or of parental responsibility? Or does it simply signal parents that they must take financial responsibility for their choices? The tendency we must resist is allowing the decision to terminate a pregnancy to become largely one of accountancy, with the expectation that if the projected financial cost is too high, the decision to abort will be administrative and routine.

These tendencies, we believe, are all-too-realistic possibilities for our future. Some are beginning to be evident even now. If they are all realized, they could constitute a nightmarish future in which any benefits that genetic technology confers would be overwhelmed by its misuses. While there is a potential for these tendencies to be realized, we do not believe they are inevitable. If they are not realized, it will be because they have been carefully considered in advance and most of all because they have been actively resisted. It is therefore a matter of the utmost urgency that churches become communities of resistance to the possible dehumanizing tendencies that could accompany the stunning technical advances of human genetics.

A Call to Affirmation

In the midst of this revolution in human procreation, what should Christians affirm about life, pain, children, and hope? What affirmations should guide our use of prenatal genetic technology?

1. *Acceptance of uncertainty.* We affirm the uncertainty, the unpredictability, and the vulnerability of life as basic to the creation and to the ways of the Creator. God has created a world in which not even God, much less we, are able to predict outcomes with certainty or to control the future with precision. There is an inherent unpredictability, even freedom, that permeates the creation at every level. We accept this as God's choice for the kind of world in which we live, and so we recognize both the scientific limits of the power of genetics and the theological limit that God has placed on all creatures to predict and to control the creation. In spite of this uncertainty and unpredictability, we must have courage to act on the basis of partial knowledge and limited power.

2. *Unconditional love.* We affirm that we are to love all creatures, especially our own children, with an unconditional acceptance that intentionally disregards any variation from any preset standard, whether social or biological. We believe that this is the kind of love God shows to us and that we are called to imitate this love.

3. *Acceptance of pain.* We affirm that we must be willing to live with pain, to take it into our lives, and not to shrink from those in pain but in appropriate ways to make their pain our own in the hope of lifting it from them. When we learn the results of a genetic test that predicts disability or painful disease, our thought will not be to isolate

ourselves from that pain but to enter into it and to respond to it with compassion rather than fear, and with self-sacrifice rather than self-protection. Above all, we affirm that we must be open to make sense of our lives within the framework of definition that God gives, between cross and resurrection, between an authentic embracing of the brokenness of our circumstances in the present and the hope of community with God at the end.

4. *Uniqueness of the fetus.* We affirm the uniqueness of each pregnancy as a distinct or special possibility for human life, recognizing that one pregnancy cannot replace another. The loss of a pregnancy for any reason is an occasion of grief. It is a time to mourn, to remember, to name, and to memorialize, and not to diminish the value of what is lost or to encourage a process of forgetting.

Pastors should recognize, with Mary Jane Dean and Mary Louise Cullen, that

> in the midst of anguish over her loss of a child, a woman does not want to hear "God's will for the design of one's life." . . . More than seeking simple answers, women want the church to affirm the baby's presence and memory and to help them reflect on their own spiritual questions. They want to be "invited to talk"—invited to think about the significance of the life that was lost.[11]

In the worship life of the congregation, grief can be expressed, the pain of the premature end of a pregnancy can be observed, and the identity of what is lost can be honored by name and in ritual.

5. *Community support.* We affirm that we need to be honest with one another about our need for the support of the Christian community, particularly when we ourselves are called upon to care for the needs of another, such as a child with a genetic condition. Parents of children with genetic conditions are often reluctant to ask for help. Pastors can help overburdened parents express their needs and encourage patterns of support within the parish community.

6. *Dignity of all persons.* We affirm the full human dignity of every human person, regardless of disability or sickness. We affirm for everyone the right of full participation and access to life in community, and we commit ourselves not only to making our congrega-

tions fully accessible but to learning to see the world through the experiences of those with disabilities.

7. *Sensitivity to those with genetic conditions.* We acknowledge the danger that those with genetic conditions will see our use of prenatal genetic testing as a threat to their existence. We affirm that special care must be taken for children in families undergoing prenatal testing, especially when those children themselves have genetic conditions, so that they not view the testing as evidence that their parents' love for them is contingent upon a criterion they can never meet.

8. *Community of the cross.* We affirm that our ultimate destiny is for community with God, and that the way to this destiny is in the company of the crucified healer. Our faith is not an anesthetic, and the cross is not a painkiller. In the community of the cross, the pain of life and death is all the more vivid, the grief all the sharper, the uncertainty all the more distressing, for there in the cross we see what pain does even to God.

9. *Hope in the resurrection.* But for this very reason we dare to hope that the God whom we know in the crucified Christ is not only present with us now in our uncertainty and suffering but will redeem our lives, our decisions, and our losses, so that in the community of the cross we will come at last to the community of the risen Christ.

Notes

Introduction

1. Ronald F. Thiemann, *Constructing a Public Theology: The Church in a Pluralistic Culture* (Louisville: Westminster John Knox, 1991), 17.

2. Ibid., 19; emphasis added.

3. James M. Gustafson, *Ethics from a Theocentric Perspective: Volume 1, Theology and Ethics* (Chicago: University of Chicago Press, 1981), 48.

4. H. Richard Niebuhr, *The Responsible Self* (New York: Harper and Row, 1963), 67.

1 Genes as a Pastoral Issue

1. George S. Hendry, *Theology of Nature* (Philadelphia: Westminster Press, 1980), 11–12.

2. World Council of Churches, *Biotechnology: Its Challenges to the Churches and the World* (Geneva: World Council of Churches, Subunit on Church and Society, 1989), 12.

3. National Council of Churches, *Genetic Science for Human Benefit* (New York: National Council of the Churches of Christ in the U.S.A., 1986), 3.

4. The United Methodist Church, *The Book of Resolutions of the United Methodist Church 1992* (Nashville, Tenn.: The United Methodist Publishing House, 1992), 336.

5. The United Church of Christ, General Synod 17, "A Pronouncement on the Church and Genetic Engineering," *Social Policy Action* (Cleveland: Office for Church in Society, United Church of Christ, 1989): 30.

6. The Congregation for the Doctrine of the Faith, "Instruction on Respect for Human Life in Its Origin and on the Dignity of Procreation," *Origins* 16 (1987): 702.

7. Ibid.

8. Ibid.

9. Hessel Bouma III, Douglas Diekema, Edward Langerak, Theodore Rottman, and Allen Verhey, *Christian Faith, Health, and Medical Practice* (Grand Rapids, Mich.: Wm. B. Eerdmans, 1989), 248.

10. Albert C. Outler, "The Beginnings of Personhood: Theological Considerations," *Perkins Journal* 27 (fall 1973): 32.

2 Through the Valley of the Shadow of Life

1. Alan H. Handyside, John G. Lesko, Juan J. Tarin, Robert M. L. Winston, and Mark R. Hughes, "Birth of a Normal Girl after In Vitro Fertilization and Preimplantation Diagnostic Testing for Cystic Fibrosis," *New England Journal of Medicine* 327 (24 September 1992): 905–10.

2. Neil A. Holtzman, *Proceed with Caution: Predicting Genetic Risks in the Recombinant DNA Era* (Baltimore: Johns Hopkins University Press, 1989), 98.

3. Abby Lippman, "The Genetic Construction of Testing: Choice, Consent, or Conformity for Women?," in *Women and Prenatal Testing: Facing the Challenges of Genetic Technology,* ed. Karen H. Rothenberg and Elizabeth J. Thomson (Columbus: Ohio State University Press, 1994), 11.

4. In 1994, a breast cancer precursor gene, BRCA1, was identified, and fairly quickly researchers learned that mutations of BRCA1 "occur in many different forms, scattered throughout the gene, making it technically challenging to develop an accurate test," according to Rachel Nowak, "Many Mutations May Make Test Difficult," *Science* 266 (2 December 1994): 1470.

5. Committee on Assessing Genetic Risks, Institute of Medicine, National Academy of Science, *Assessing Genetic Risks: Implications for Health and Social Policy,* ed. Lori B. Andrews, Jane E. Fullarton, Neil A. Holtzman, and Arno G. Motulsky (Washington, D.C.: National Academy Press, 1994), 37.

6. Ibid., 96.

7. Ibid., 164.

8. Ibid., 166.

9. For a review of research on tandem repeat genetic conditions, see Stephen T. Warren and Claude T. Ashley Jr., "Triplet Repeat Expansion Mutations: The Example of Fragile X Syndrome," *Annual Review of Neuroscience* 18 (1995): 77–99.

10. Robert F. Service, "Stalking the Start of Colon Cancer," *Science* 263 (18 March 1994): 1559.

11. S. D. Merajver, T. M. Pham, R. F. Caduff, M. Chen, E. L. Poy, K. A. Cooney, B. L. Weber, F. S. Collins, C. Johnston, and T. S. Frank, "Somatic Conditions in the BRCA1 Gene in Sporadic Ovarian Tumours," *Nature Genetics* 9 (April 1995): 432–39.

12. A study of the emotional impact of being tested for Huntington's disease suggests that relief over knowing one's status may outweigh the negative consequences, at least until symptoms begin to develop. See A. Tibben et al., "Psychological Effects of Presymptomatic DNA Testing for Huntington's Disease in the Dutch Program," *Psychosomatic Medicine* 56 (November–December 1994): 526–32.

13. E. H. Corder, A. M. Saunders, W. J. Strittmatter, D. E. Schmechel, P. C. Gaskell, G. W. Small, A. D. Roses, J. L. Haines, and M. A. Pericak-Vance, "Gene Dose of Apolipoprotein E Type 4 Allele and the Risk of Alzheimer's Disease in Late Onset Families," *Science* 261 (13 August 1993): 921–23.

14. Beth A. Fine, "The Evolution of Nondirectiveness in Genetic Counseling and Implications of the Human Genome Project," in *Prescribing Our Future: Ethical Challenges in Genetic Counseling,* ed. Dianne M. Bartels, Bonnie S. LeRoy, and Arthur L. Caplan (Hawthorne, N.Y.: Aldine de Gruyter, 1993), 111.

15. Kinneret Savitsky, Anat Bar-Shira, Shlomit Gilad, et al., "A Single Ataxia Telangiectasia Gene with a Product Similar to Pl-3 Kinase," *Science* 268 (23 June 1995): 1749–53.

3   The Pastor's Role

1. Committee on Assessing Genetic Risks, *Assessing Genetic Risks,* 4.

2. Cf. Charles L. Bosk, *All God's Mistakes: Genetic Counseling in a Pediatric Hospital* (Chicago: University of Chicago Press, 1992), for a discussion of the work of pediatricians as genetic counselors.

3. Committee on Assessing Genetic Risks, *Assessing Genetic Risks,* 168.

4. Ibid., 170.

5. Marc Lappe, "Risk and the Ethics of Genetic Choice," in *Prescribing Our Future: Ethical Challenges in Genetic Counseling,* ed. Dianne M. Bartels, Bonnie S. LeRoy, and Arthur L. Caplan (Hawthorne, N.Y.: Aldine de Gruyter, 1993), 61.

6. Ibid., 62.

7. Ibid., 58.

8. Ibid., 61.

9. Barbara Katz Rothman, "Not All That Glitters Is Gold," *Hastings Center Report* (Special Supplement, July–August 1992): S12–13.

10. Kathleen Nolan, "First Fruits: Genetic Screening," *Hastings Center Report* (Special Supplement, July–August, 1992): S4.

11. Bosk, *All God's Mistakes,* 63.

12. Ibid., 64.

13. Rothman, "Not All That Glitters," S13.

14. Rose Green [pseud.], "Letter to a Genetic Counselor," *Journal of Genetic Counseling* 1 (1992): 60.

15. Rothman, "Not All That Glitters," S13.

16. Green, "Letter to a Genetic Counselor," 69.

17. Dorothy Wertz and John Fletcher, "Attitudes of Genetic Counselors: A Multinational Survey," *American Journal of Human Genetics* 42 (1988): 592–600.

18. Committee on Assessing Genetic Risks, *Assessing Genetic Risks,* 152.

19. Arthur L. Caplan, "Neutrality Is Not Morality: The Ethics of Genetic Counseling," in *Prescribing Our Future: Ethical Challenges in Genetic Counseling,* ed. Dianne M. Bartels, Bonnie S. LeRoy, and Arthur L. Caplan (Hawthorne, N.Y.: Aldine de Gruyter, 1993), 162.

20. Karen Grandstrand Gervais, "Objectivity, Value Neutrality, and Nondirectiveness in Genetic Counseling," in *Prescribing Our Future: Ethical Challenges in Genetic Counseling,* ed. Dianne M. Bartels, Bonnie S. LeRoy, and Arthur L. Caplan (Hawthorne, N.Y.: Aldine de Gruyter, 1993), 119.

21. Ibid., 124.

22. Ibid., 126.

23. Ibid., 126–27.

24. Ibid., 127.

25. Committee on Assessing Genetic Risks, *Assessing Genetic Risks,* 155.

26. Ibid., 154.

27. Caplan, "Neutrality Is Not Morality," 160.

28. National Society of Genetics Counselors, "National Society of Genetic Counselors Code of Ethics," *Journal of Genetic Counseling* 1 (1992): 42.

29. Committee on Assessing Genetic Risks, *Assessing Genetic Risks,* 16.

30. "Principles," in *Genetic Counseling Principles in Action: A Casebook,* ed. Joan H. Marks, Audrey Heimler, Elsa Reich, Nancy S. Wexler, and Susan E. Ince (White Plains, N.Y.: March of Dimes Birth Defects Foundation, 1989), 138, 140.

31. Jodi K. Rucquoi and M. J. Mahoney, "A Protocol to Address the Depressive Effects of Abortion for Fetal Abnormalities Discovered Prenatally via Amniocentesis," in *Psychosocial Aspects of Genetic Counseling,* March of Dimes Birth Defects Foundation Original Article Series, vol. 28, no. 1, ed. Gerry Evers-Kiebooms, Jean-Pierre Fryns, Jean-Jacques Cassiman, and Herman Van den Berghe (New York: John Wiley, 1992), 58.

32. John C. Fletcher, *Coping with Genetic Disorders: A Guide for Clergy and Parents* (San Francisco: Harper and Row, 1982), 33–49, speaks of the clergy role as the offering of "faithful companionship." We prefer the term "theological companionship" because it stresses the unique identity of the pastoral caregiver.

33. Ibid., 41

34. Green, "Letter to a Genetic Counselor," 61

35. Rothman, "Not All That Glitters," S13.

4   Making a Baby: From Procreation to Reproduction

1. As quoted in National Center for Human Genome Research Office, Office of Communications, "Human Genome Progress" (press release), 16 November 1990.

2. Leon Kass, *Toward a More Natural Science: Biology and Human Affairs* (New York: Free Press, 1985), 173.

3. Walter E. Nance, "Parables," in *Prescribing Our Future: Ethical Challenges in Genetic Counseling,* ed. Dianne M. Bartels, Bonnie S. LeRoy, and Arthur L. Caplan (Hawthorne, N.Y.: Aldine de Gruyter, 1993), 91.

4. Ibid., 92.

5. Christopher Lasch, "Engineering the Good Life: The Search for Perfection," *This World* 26 (summer 1989): 9.

6. Troy Duster, "Genetics, Race, and Crime: Recurring Seduction to a False Precision," in *DNA on Trial: Genetic Identification and Criminal Justice,* ed. Paul R. Billings (Cold Springs Harbor, N.Y.: Cold Springs Harbor Laboratory Press, 1992), 133.

7. Ibid., 139.

8. H. G. Brunner, M. Nelen, X. O. Breakefield, H. H. Ropers, and B. A. van Oost, "Abnormal Behavior Associated with a Point Mutation in the Structural Gene for Monoamine Oxidase A," *Science* 262 (22 October 1993): 578–80. As of mid-1995, no additional families with this condition have been found. However, researchers have altered the analogous gene in mice and the affected mice exhibited strikingly similar behavior results. In addition, when the researchers treated some of the genetically altered mice, beginning at birth, they eliminated many of the behaviors. Cf. Olivier Cases, Isabelle Seif, Joseph Grimsby, et al., "Aggressive Behavior and Altered Amounts of Brain Serotonin and Norepinephrine in Mice Lacking MAOA," *Science* 268 (23 June 1995): 1763–66.

9. Virginia Morell, "Evidence Found for a Possible 'Aggression Gene,'" *Science* 260 (18 June 1993): 1722–23.

10. As an example, see Dean H. Hamer, Stella Hu, Victoria L. Magnuson, Nan Hu, and Angela M. L. Pattatucci, "A Linkage between DNA Markers on the X Chromosome and Male Sexual Orientation," *Science* 261 (16 July 1993): 321–27. This study found a relationship between a region of the X chromosome and male homosexuality. As of mid-1995, the study is only beginning to be replicated, and its technical merits have been both sharply criticized and defended by other researchers. Genetic twin studies do indicate that genes play a significant but only partial role in explaining sexual orientation.

11. Cf. Ronald S. Cole-Turner, "The Genetics of Moral Agency," in *The Genetic Frontier: Ethics, Law, and Policy,* ed. Mark S. Frankel and Albert Teich (Washington, D.C.: American Association for the Advancement of Science, 1994), 161–74; and Ted Peters, *Sin: Radical Evil in Soul and Society* (Grand Rapids, Mich.: Wm. B. Eerdmans, 1994), 294–327.

12. See Richard John Neuhaus, ed., *Guaranteeing the Good Life: Medicine and the Return of Eugenics* (Grand Rapids, Mich.: Wm. B. Eerdmans, 1990).

13. Elizabeth Kristol, "Picture Perfect: The Politics of Prenatal Testing," *First Things* 32 (April 1993): 17.

14. Ibid., 24.

15. Lippman, "The Genetic Construction of Testing," 22–23.

16. Committee on Assessing Genetic Risks, *Assessing Genetic Risks,* 15.

17. Robert H. Blank, *Life, Death, and Public Policy* (DeKalb: Northern Illinois University Press, 1988), 39.

18. Ibid.

19. Ruth Schwartz Cowan, "Genetic Technology and Reproductive Choice: An Ethics of Autonomy," in *The Code of Codes: Scientific and Social*

Issues in the Human Genome Project, ed. Daniel J. Kevles and Leroy Hood (Cambridge, Mass.: Harvard University Press, 1992), 262.

20. Ibid.

21. John Robertson, "Procreative Liberty and the Control of Conception, Pregnancy, and Childbirth," *Virginia Law Review* 69 (April 1983): 430.

22. Maura A. Ryan, "The Argument for Unlimited Procreative Liberty: A Feminist Critique," in *Bioethics: Basic Writings on the Key Ethical Questions That Surround the Major, Modern Biological Possibilities and Problems,* 4th ed., ed. Thomas A. Shannon (Mahwah, N.J.: Paulist Press, 1993), 84. This essay was first published in *Hastings Center Report* 20 (July/August 1990): 6–12.

23. Ibid., 85.

24. Patricia Spallone, *Beyond Conception: The New Politics of Reproduction* (Granby, Conn.: Bergin and Garvey, 1989), 184.

25. Ibid.

26. Ibid., 192–93.

27. Ibid., 193.

28. Maria Mies, "'Why Do We Need All This? A Call against Genetic Engineering and Reproductive Technology," in *Made to Order: The Myth of Reproductive and Genetic Progress,* ed. Patricia Spallone and Deborah Lynn Steinberg (Oxford, Eng.: Pergamon Press, 1987), 35.

29. Ibid., 37; cf. George Parkin Grant, *Technology and Justice* (Notre Dame, Ind.: University of Notre Dame Press, 1986), 11–34.

30. Ibid., 45.

31. Ibid., 46.

32. Barbara Katz Rothman, "The Tentative Pregnancy: Then and Now," in *Women and Prenatal Testing: Facing the Challenges of Genetic Technology,* ed. Karen H. Rothenberg and Elizabeth J. Thomson (Columbus: Ohio State University Press, 1994), 263.

33. Ibid.

34. Lippman, "The Genetic Construction of Testing," 29.

35. John A. Robertson, *Children of Choice: Freedom and the New Reproductive Technologies.* (Princeton, N.J.: Princeton University Press, 1994), 235.

36. Ibid.

37. Ted Peters, "Designer Children: The Market World of Reproductive Choice," *Christian Century* 14 (December 1994): 1196.

38. Oliver O'Donovan, *Begotten or Made?* (Oxford, Eng.: Clarendon Press, 1984), 2.

39. Ibid., 12.

40. Ibid.

41. At this point O'Donovan's conclusions (but not the premises!) are remarkably similar to those of Barbara Katz Rothman, who in criticizing reproductive technology, writes: "The technology we develop grows out of this constructed contractual way of thinking, this perception of babies not as growing out of their mothers, flesh of their flesh, part of their lives, bodies, and communities, but as separating beings implanted within." In Rothman, "The Tentative Pregnancy," 264.

42. Stanley Hauerwas, *Suffering Presence: Theological Reflections on Medicine, the Mentally Handicapped, and the Church* (Notre Dame, Ind.: University of Notre Dame Press, 1986), 145.

43. Ibid., 146.

44. Ibid., 149.

45. O'Donovan, *Begotten or Made?*, 47.

46. Hauerwas, *Suffering Presence,* 160.

47. Ibid., 168.

48. Stanley Hauerwas, with Richard Bondi and David B. Burrell, *Truthfulness and Tragedy: Further Investigations into Christian Ethics* (Notre Dame, Ind.: University of Notre Dame Press, 1977), 196.

49. See Paul Ramsey, *The Patient as Person: Explorations in Medical Ethics* (New Haven, Conn.: Yale University Press, 1970); cf. William F. May, *The Physician's Covenant: Images of the Healer in Medical Ethics* (Philadelphia: The Westminster Press, 1983), 87–105.

50. Hauerwas, *Suffering Presence,* 150.

51. Paul Ramsey, *Fabricated Man: The Ethics of Genetic Control* (New Haven, Conn.: Yale University Press, 1970), 159.

52. Iris Murdoch, *Acastos: Two Platonic Dialogues* (London: Penguin Books, 1986), 73.

53. Ramsey, *Fabricated Man,* 160

54. See Oliver O'Donovan, *Resurrection and Moral Order: An Outline for Evangelical Ethics* (Grand Rapids, Mich.: Wm. B. Eerdmans, 1986), 31–52.

55. Ronald Cole-Turner, *The New Genesis: Theology and the Genetic Revolution* (Louisville: Westminster John Knox, 1993), 80–97.

56. Gena Corea, *Mother Machine: Reproductive Technologies from Artificial Insemination to Artificial Wombs* (New York: Harper and Row, 1985), 314.

57. Ibid., 285.

58. Ibid., 303.

5   Creation and Procreation: Connecting God with Genetic Processes

1. This point has been made with great force and clarity by Wolfhart Pannenberg, *Systematic Theology,* vol. 1, trans. Geoffrey W. Bromiley (Grand Rapids, Mich.: Wm. B. Eerdmans, 1991).

2. Gustafson, *Ethics from a Theocentric Perspective: Vol. 1,* 5.

3. Ibid., 48.

4. Ibid., 25.

5. Ibid., 210.

6. Ibid., 264.

7. Ibid., 262.

8. Ibid., 240.

9. Ibid., 241.

10. Ibid.

11. Ibid., 248.

12. Ibid., 248–49.

13. Ibid., 249.

14. Ibid.

15. Ibid., 48.

16. Arthur Peacocke, *God and the New Biology* (London: Dent, 1986), 96.

17. Among the philosophers is mathematician D. J. Bartholomew, whose *God of Chance* (London: SCM Press, 1984) is one of the first sustained challenges to the philosophical and theological implications of Monod.

18. Arthur Peacocke, *Theology for a Scientific Age: Being and Becoming—Natural, Divine and Human* (Minneapolis: Fortress Press, 1993), 117.

19. Ibid., 118.

20. Ibid.

21. Ibid.

22. Ibid., 119; cf. Peacocke, *God and the New Biology,* 97.

23. Ibid.

24. Peacocke, *God and the New Biology,* 99.

25. Arthur Peacocke, *Creation and the World of Science* (Oxford, Eng.: Clarendon Press, 1979), 230.

26. Peacocke, *Theology for a Scientific Age,* 126.

27. John C. Polkinghorne, *One World* (Princeton, N.J.: Princeton University Press, 1986), 67.

28. Robert J. Russell's typescript paper, "Theistic Evolution: Does God Really Act in Nature?", was presented in August 1994 at a consultation on theology and genetics at the Evangelische Akademie Loccum, Germany. It is being revised for publication. The pages that follow are deeply indebted to Russell's thinking, drawn from his paper, personal conversation, and correspondence.

29. Russell observes that Peacocke's position depends upon the universe having a beginning in time. Currently, Big Bang cosmology suggests such a beginning. But scientific cosmology is a dynamic field of research, and future proposals in cosmology may not included a beginning in time.

30. Russell, "Theistic Evolution," 14, emphasis in original. For the argument, see Robert J. Russell, "Quantum Physics in Philosophical and Theological Perspective," in *Physics, Philosophy, and Theology: A Common Quest for Understanding*, ed. R. J. Russell, W. R. Stoeger, and C. V. Coyne (Notre Dame, Ind.: University of Notre Dame Press, 1988), 343–74.

31. Russell, "Theistic Evolution," 15.

32. Mary Potter Engel, *John Calvin's Perspectival Anthropology* (Atlanta: Scholars Press, 1988), 127; the original is in Calvin's commentary on Amos 4.

33. Ibid.

34. Russell (personal correspondence) comments on his proposal in relation to a traditional theological understanding of divine providence, affirming a limited notion of special providence: "We can put this claim in traditional language by stating that God's general providence includes the sustaining of the universe in being, moment by moment, and its lawlike regularity; whereas God's special providence involves God acting in certain key events that shape the creation and salvation of the world. Quantum indeterminacy, and with it the genotype-phenotype relationship, provides one of the many ways in which special providence can be understood as compatible with contemporary science, despite the claims of Monod and others that this is impossible."

35. Russell, personal correspondence (see note 34).

6   The Presence of God in Pain

1. We note with some amazement that in a recent book by Eric J. Cassell, entitled *The Nature of Suffering and the Goals of Medicine* (New York: Oxford University Press, 1991), only a brief, three-paragraph subsection is devoted to "The Nature of Suffering," and it lacks anything resembling a definition (pp. 43–44). This confirms the earlier assessment made by

Stanley Hauerwas, *Suffering Presence,* 29: "After trying to read all I could get my hands on concerning the meaning of suffering, I am convinced that never has there been a word used with such an uncritical assumption that everyone knows what they are talking about."

2. Hauerwas, *Suffering Presence,* 165.

3. Ibid., 181.

4. Paul Fiddes, *The Creative Suffering of God* (Oxford: Clarendon Press, 1988), 11.

5. Jürgen Moltmann, *The Crucified God: The Cross of Christ as the Foundation and Criticism of Christian Theology,* trans. R. A. Wilson and John Bowden (New York: Harper and Row, 1974), 4.

6. Jürgen Moltmann, *The Trinity and the Kingdom: The Doctrine of God,* trans. Margaret Kohl (New York: Harper and Row, 1981), 49.

7. Fiddes, *The Creative Suffering of God,* 16.

8. Ibid., 17.

9. Moltmann, *The Crucified God,* 245.

10. Ibid., 207.

11. Ibid., 246.

12. Ibid.

13. Ibid., 40.

14. A helpful approach to this question is taken by Nancy L. Eiesland, *The Disabled God: Toward a Liberatory Theology of Disability* (Nashville, Tenn.: Abingdon Press, 1994).

15. Simone Weil, *Intimations of Christianity among the Ancient Greeks,* ed. and trans. Elisabeth Chase Geissbuhler (London: Routledge and Kegan Paul, 1957), 60, 65.

16. Moltmann, *The Crucified God.*

17. I [RCT] cannot help but recall the story told by a seminarian, Linda Woods, who had been a neonatal intensive care nurse. She permitted herself to become attached to an infant born with trisomy 18, a serious chromosomal disorder that leads to death within a few months. Ms. Woods wanted to take the infant, a girl whom she named Abby, into her home as a foster child. At first the state objected to a first-time foster mother taking a "special" child. Friends intervened, and Abby's brief life had the extraordinary effect of opening Ms. Woods's relationship with God so that "Abby" became, as she recognized only later, her access to "Abba." Through her weakness, Abby transformed the one with power, the medical professional, by bringing her into a community of healing beyond power. See Linda Wood, "A Glimpse of Grace," *The Cumberland Seminarian* 23, no. 1–2 (fall/spring 1985): 7–10.

18. Stanley Hauerwas, *Naming the Silences: God, Medicine, and the Problem of Suffering* (Grand Rapids, Mich.: Wm. B. Eerdmans, 1990), 126–51.

19. Ibid., 62.

20. Hauerwas, *Suffering Presence*, 17.

21. Ibid.

22. Ramsey, *Fabricated Man*, 134.

23. See James W. McClendon Jr., *Doctrine: Systematic Theology*, vol. 2 (Nashville, Tenn.: Abingdon Press, 1994), 146–89.

24. Ibid., 162.

25. Ibid., 166.

26. Ibid. Cf. Philip Hefner, *The Human Factor: Evolution, Culture, and Religion* (Minneapolis: Fortress Press, 1993), 55–94.

27. Ibid., 167–68.

28. Ibid., 168.

29. Cf. ibid., 171–76.

30. Ibid., 169.

31. Ibid.

32. Green, "Letter to a Genetic Counselor," 61.

7   Human Genetics in Light of the Resurrection

1 For discussion of the biblical and historical issues regarding the resurrection, see Peter Carnley, *The Structure of Resurrection Belief* (Oxford, Eng.: Clarendon Press, 1987), 16–95.

2. See J. Christiaan Beker, *Paul the Apostle: The Triumph of God in Life and Thought* (Edinburgh: T & T Clark, 1980), 135–81.

3. Ibid., 180–81.

4. John Polkinghorne, *The Faith of a Physicist: Reflections of a Bottom-Up Thinker, The Gifford Lectures for 1993–94* (Princeton, N.J.: Princeton University Press, 1994), 90.

5. Ibid., 89.

6. See Oscar Cullmann, *Immortality of the Soul or Resurrection of the Dead?: The Witness of the New Testament* (London: Epworth Press, 1958).

7. Cf. Caroline Walker Bynum, *The Resurrection of the Body in Western Christianity* (New York: Columbia University Press, 1995), 200–1336

8. Wolfhart Pannenberg, *Systematic Theology*, vol. 2, trans. Geoffrey W. Bromiley (Grand Rapids, Mich.: Wm. B. Eerdmans, 1994), 182.

9. See Carnley, *The Structure of Resurrection Belief,* 96–147.

10. John Macquarrie, *Jesus Christ in Modern Thought* (Philadelphia: Trinity Press International, 1990), 406.

11. See Carnley, *The Structure of Resurrection Belief,* 148–82.

12. Polkinghorne, *The Faith of a Physicist,* 109.

13. Jaroslav Pelikan, *Christianity and Classical Culture: The Metamorphosis of Natural Theology in the Christian Encounter with Hellenism, The Gifford Lectures, 1992–1993* (New Haven, Conn.: Yale University Press, 1993).

14. Wolfhart Pannenberg, *The Apostles' Creed: In the Light of Today's Questions,* trans. Margaret Kohl (Philadelphia: Westminster Press, 1972), 96.

15. Moltmann, *Theology of Hope,* 172–73.

16. Pannenberg, *The Apostles' Creed,* 97.

17. Jürgen Moltmann, *The Way of Jesus Christ: Christology in Messianic Dimensions,* trans. Margaret Kohl (San Francisco: HarperCollins, 1990), 213.

18. Pannenberg, *The Apostles' Creed,* 170.

19. Moltmann, *The Way of Jesus Christ,* 272.

20. Polkinghorne, *The Faith of a Physicist,* 161.

21. O'Donovan, *Resurrection and Moral Order,* 13.

22. Ibid., 258.

23. Ibid.

24. Ibid., 259.

25. Ibid.

26. Ibid., 260.

27. Ibid.

28. Pannenberg, *Systematic Theology,* 200.

29. Joyce Irwin, "Embryology and the Incarnation: A Sixteenth-Century Debate," *Sixteenth Century Journal* 9 (1978): 92–104.

30. Here we include embryo research, including germline manipulation, which introduces genetic changes that would be passed indefinitely to future generations.

31. Lisa Sowle Cahill, "The Embryo and the Fetus: New Moral Contexts," *Theological Studies* 54 (1993): 124.

32. Cf. Hans-Martin Sass, "Brain Life and Brain Death, *Journal of Medicine and Philosophy* 14 (1989): 45–59.

33. Mario Moussa and Thomas A Shannon, "The Search for the New Pineal Gland: Brain Life and Personhood," *Hastings Center Report* 22 (1992): 30–31.

34. Ibid., 36.

35. Ibid.

36. Outler, "The Beginnings of Personhood," 31.

37. Pannenberg, *Systematic Theology,* vol. 2, 176.

38. Ibid., 177.

39. Ibid., 224.

40. Ibid., 200.

41. Ibid., 201.

42. Augustine of Hippo, "City of God," in *A Select Library of the Nicene and Post-Nicene Fathers of the Christian Church,* vol. 2, ed. Philip Schaff (Buffalo, N.Y.: Christian Literature Co., 1887), 499.

43. Ibid., 497.

44. Ibid., 495.

45. Ibid., 498.

46. Ibid., 495.

47. Ibid.

48. Ibid., 494.

49. Augustine, "City of God," trans. Henry Bettenson (London: Penguin Books, 1972), Book XXII.14, 1055.

50. Ibid., Book XXII.19, 1061.

51. Gregory of Nyssa, "On Infants' Early Deaths," trans. William Moore and Henry Austin Wilson, in *Select Writings and Letters of Gregory, Bishop of Nyssa: A Select Library of Nicene and Post-Nicene Fathers of the Christian Church,* second series, vol. 5, ed. Philip Schaff and Henry Wace (Grand Rapids, Mich.: Wm. B. Eerdmans, 1979), 373–74.

52. Austin Farrer, *Love Almighty and Ills Unlimited* (Garden City, N.Y.: Doubleday, 1961), 166.

53. Polkinghorne, *The Faith of a Physicist,* 12.

54. Pannenberg, *Systematic Theology,* vol. 2, 202.

55. For an extended discussion of the seed metaphor in 1 Cor. 15, see J. A. Schep, *The Nature of the Resurrection Body: A Study of the Biblical Data* (Grand Rapids, Mich.: Wm. B. Eerdmans, 1964), 192–210; and Bynum, *The Resurrection of the Body,* 27–43.

56. Polkinghorne, *The Faith of a Physicist,* 121–22.

57. James D. G. Dunn, *Romans 1–8* (Dallas: Word Books, 1988), 471.

58. Ibid., 473.

59. Ibid., 467.

60. Polkinghorne, *The Faith of a Physicist,* 164.

61. Ibid., 167.

62. Ibid., 164.

63. See Marjorie Hewitt Suchocki, *The End of Evil: Process Eschatology in Historical Context* (Albany: State University of New York Press, 1988).

8   The Vocation of Prenatal Parenting

1. O'Donovan, *Resurrection and Moral Order,* 259–60.

2. Quoted in Robert Rankin, "Beginnings," in *The Recovery of Spirit in Higher Education: Christian and Jewish Ministries in Campus Life,* ed. Robert Rankin (New York: Seabury Press, 1980), 10.

3. Outler, "The Beginnings of Personhood," 32.

4. Kristol, "Picture Perfect," 21.

5. Quoted in Kristol, "Picture Perfect," 22.

6. Hamer et al., "Linkage between DNA Markers," 321–27.

7. Kristol, "Picture Perfect," 21.

8. Ibid.

9. Quoted in Kristol, "Picture Perfect," 23.

10. Cf. Eiesland, *The Disabled God.*

11. Mary Jane Dean and Mary Louise Cullen, "Woman's Body: Spiritual Needs and Theological Presence," in *Women in Travail and Transition: A New Pastoral Care,* ed. Maxine Glaz and Jeanne Stevenson Moessner (Minneapolis: Augsburg Fortress Press, 1991), 96.

Bibliography

Augustine of Hippo. "City of God." In *A Select Library of the Nicene and Post-Nicene Fathers of the Christian Church,* vol. 2, edited by Philip Schaff. Buffalo, N.Y.: Christian Literature Co., 1887.

Bartholomew, D. J. *God of Chance.* London: SCM Press, 1984.

Beker, J. Christiaan. *Paul the Apostle: The Triumph of God in Life and Thought.* Edinburgh: T & T Clark, 1980.

Blank, Robert H. *Life, Death, and Public Policy.* DeKalb: Northern Illinois University Press, 1988.

Bosk, Charles L. *All God's Mistakes: Genetic Counseling in a Pediatric Hospital.* Chicago: University of Chicago Press, 1992.

Bouma, Hessel, III, Douglas Diekema, Edward Langerak, Theodore Rottman, and Allen Verhey. *Christian Faith, Health, and Medical Practice.* Grand Rapids, Mich.: Wm. B. Eerdmans, 1989.

Brunner, H. G., M. Nelen, X. O. Breakefield. H. H. Ropers, and B. A. van Oost. "Abnormal Behavior Associated with a Point Mutation in the Structural Gene for Monoamine Oxidase A." *Science* 262 (22 October 1993): 578–80.

Bynum, Caroline Walker. *The Resurrection of the Body in Western Christianity.* New York: Columbia University Press, 1995.

Cahill, Lisa Sowle. "The Embryo and the Fetus: New Moral Contexts." *Theological Studies* 54 (1993): 124–42.

Caplan, Arthur L. "Neutrality Is Not Morality: The Ethics of Genetic Counseling." In *Prescribing Our Future: Ethical Challenges in Genetic Counseling,* edited by Dianne M. Bartels, Bonnie S. LeRoy, and Arthur L. Caplan. Hawthorne, N.Y.: Aldine de Gruyter, 1993.

Carnley, Peter. *The Structure of Resurrection Belief.* Oxford, Eng.: Clarendon Press, 1987.

Cases, Olivier, Isabelle Seif, Joseph Grimsby, et al. "Aggressive Behavior and Altered Amounts of Brain Serotonin and Norepinephrine in Mice Lacking MAOA." *Science* 268 (23 June 1995): 1763–66.

Cassell, Eric J. *The Nature of Suffering and the Goals of Medicine.* New York: Oxford University Press, 1991.

Cole-Turner, Ronald. "The Genetics of Moral Agency." *The Genetic Frontier: Ethics, Law, and Policy.* Edited by Mark S. Frankel and Albert Teich. Washington, D.C.: American Association for the Advancement of Science, 1994.

————. *The New Genesis: Theology and the Genetic Revolution.* Louisville: Westminster John Knox, 1993.

Committee on Assessing Genetic Risks, Institute of Medicine, National Academy of Science. *Assessing Genetic Risks: Implications for Health and Social Policy.* Edited by Lori B. Andrews, Jane E. Fullarton, Neil A. Holtzman, and Arno G. Motulsky. Washington, D.C.: National Academy Press, 1994.

Congregation for the Doctrine of the Faith. "Instruction on Respect for Human Life in Its Origin and on the Dignity of Procreation." *Origins* 16 (1987): 702.

Corder, E. H., A. M. Saunders, W. J. Strittmatter, D. E. Schmechel, P. C. Gaskell, G. W. Small, A. D. Roses, J. L. Haines, and M. A. Pericak-Vance. "Gene Dose of Apolipoprotein E Type 4 Allele and the Risk of Alzheimer's Disease in Late Onset Families." *Science* 261 (13 August 1993): 921–23.

Corea, Gena. *Mother Machine: Reproductive Technologies from Artificial Insemination to Artificial Wombs.* New York: Harper and Row, 1985.

Cowan, Ruth Schwartz. "Genetic Technology and Reproductive Choice: An Ethics of Autonomy. In *The Code of Codes: Scientific and Social Issues in the Human Genome Project,* edited by Daniel J. Kevles and Leroy Hood. Cambridge, Mass.: Harvard University Press, 1992.

Cullmann, Oscar. *Immortality of the Soul or Resurrection of the Dead?: The Witness of the New Testament.* London: Epworth Press, 1958.

Dean, Mary Jane, and Mary Louise Cullen. "Woman's Body: Spiritual Needs and Theological Presence." In *Women in Travail and Transition: A New Pastoral Care,* edited by Maxine Glaz and Jeanne Stevenson Moessner. Minneapolis: Augsburg Fortress Press, 1991.

Dunn, James D. G. *Romans 1–8.* Dallas, Tex.: Word Books, 1988.

Duster, Troy. "Genetics, Race, and Crime: Recurring Seduction to a False Precision." In *DNA on Trial: Genetic Identification and Criminal Justice,* edited by Paul R. Billings. Cold Springs Harbor, N.Y.: Cold Springs Harbor Laboratory Press, 1992.

Eiesland, Nancy L. *The Disabled God: Toward a Liberatory Theology of Disability.* Nashville, Tenn.: Abingdon Press, 1994.

Engel, Mary Potter. *John Calvin's Perspectival Anthropology.* Atlanta: Scholars Press, 1988.

Farrer, Austin. *Love Almighty and Ills Unlimited.* Garden City, N.Y.: Doubleday, 1961.

Fiddes, Paul. *The Creative Suffering of God.* Oxford, Eng.: Clarendon Press, 1988.

Fine, Beth A. "The Evolution of Nondirectiveness in Genetic Counseling and Implications of the Human Genome Project." In *Prescribing Our Future: Ethical Challenges in Genetic Counseling,* edited by Dianne M. Bartels, Bonnie S. LeRoy, and Arthur L. Caplan. Hawthorne, N.Y.: Aldine de Gruyter, 1993.

Fletcher, John C. *Coping with Genetic Disorders: A Guide for Clergy and Parents.* San Francisco: Harper and Row, 1982.

Gervais, Karen Grandstrand. "Objectivity, Value Neutrality, and Nondirectiveness in Genetic Counseling." In *Prescribing Our Future: Ethical Challenges In Genetic Counseling,* edited by Dianne M. Bartels, Bonnie S. LeRoy, and Arthur L. Caplan. Hawthorne, N.Y.: Aldine de Gruyter, 1993.

Green, Rose [pseud.]. "Letter to a Genetic Counselor." *Journal of Genetic Counseling* 1 (1992): 55–70.

Gregory of Nyssa. "On Infants' Early Deaths." Trans. William Moore and Henry Austin Wilson. In *Select Writings and Letters of Gregory, Bishop of Nyssa, A Select Library of Nicene and Post-Nicene Fathers of the Christian Church,* second series, vol. 5, edited by Philip Schaff and Henry Wace. Grand Rapids, Mich.: Wm. B. Eerdmans, 1979.

Gustafson, James M. *Ethics from a Theocentric Perspective. Vol. 1. Theology and Ethics.* Chicago: University of Chicago Press, 1981.

Hamer, Dean H., Stella Hu, Victoria L. Magnuson, Nan Hu, and Angela M. L. Pattatucci. "A Linkage between DNA Markers on the X Chromosome and Male Sexual Orientation." *Science* 261 (16 July 1993): 321–27.

Handyside, Alan H., John G. Lesko, Juan J. Tarin, Robert M. L. Winston, and Mark R. Hughes. "Birth of a Normal Girl after In Vitro Fertilization and Preimplantation Diagnostic Testing for Cystic Fibrosis." *New England Journal of Medicine* 327 (24 September 1992): 905–10 .

Hauerwas, Stanley. *Naming the Silences: God, Medicine, and the Problem of Suffering.* Grand Rapids, Mich.: Wm. B. Eerdmans, 1990.

————. *Suffering Presence: Theological Reflections on Medicine, the Mentally Handicapped, and the Church.* Notre Dame, Ind.: University of Notre Dame Press, 1986.

Hauerwas, Stanley, with Richard Bondi and David B. Burrell. *Truthfulness and Tragedy: Further Investigations into Christian Ethics.* Notre Dame, Ind.: University of Notre Dame Press, 1977.

Hefner, Philip. *The Human Factor: Evolution, Culture, and Religion.* Minneapolis: Fortress Press, 1993.

Hendry, George S. *Theology of Nature.* Philadelphia: Westminster Press, 1980.

Holtzman, Neil A. *Proceed with Caution: Predicting Genetic Risks in the Recombinant DNA Era.* Baltimore: Johns Hopkins University Press, 1989.

Irwin, Joyce. "Embryology and the Incarnation: A Sixteenth-Century Debate." *Sixteenth Century Journal* 9 (1978): 92–104.

Kass, Leon. *Toward a More Natural Science: Biology and Human Affairs.* New York: Free Press, 1985.

Kristol, Elizabeth. "Picture Perfect: The Politics of Prenatal Testing." *First Things* 32 (April 1993):21.

Lappe, Marc. "Risk and the Ethics of Genetic Choice." In *Prescribing Our Future: Ethical Challenges in Genetic Counseling,* edited by Dianne M. Bartels, Bonnie S. LeRoy, and Arthur L. Caplan. Hawthorne, N.Y.: Aldine de Gruyter, 1993.

Lasch, Christopher. "Engineering the Good Life: The Search for Perfection." *This World* 26 (summer 1989): 9–17.

Lippman, Abby. "The Genetic Construction of Prenatal Testing: Choice, Consent, or Conformity for Women?" In *Women and Prenatal Testing: Facing the Challenges of Genetic Technology,* edited by Karen H. Rothenberg and Elizabeth J. Thomson. Columbus: Ohio State University Press, 1994.

Macquarrie, John. *Jesus Christ in Modern Thought.* Philadelphia: Trinity Press International, 1990.

McClendon, James W., Jr. *Doctrine: Systematic Theology,* vol. 2. Nashville, Tenn.: Abingdon Press, 1994.

Merajver, S. D., T. M. Pham, R. F. Caduff, M. Chen, E. L. Poy, K. A. Cooney, B. L. Weber, F. S. Collins, C. Johnston, and T. S. Frank. "Somatic Conditions in the BRCA1 Gene in Sporadic Ovarian Tumours." *Nature Genetics* 9 (April 1995): 432–39.

Mies, Maria. "Why Do We Need All This? A Call against Genetic Engineering and Reproductive Technology." In *Made to Order: The*

Myth of Reproductive and Genetic Progress, edited by Patricia Spallone and Deborah Lynn Steinberg. Oxford, Eng.: Pergamon Press, 1987.

Moltmann, Jürgen. *The Crucified God: The Cross of Christ as the Foundation and Criticism of Christian Theology.* Trans. R. A. Wilson and John Bowden. New York: Harper and Row, 1974.

———. *Theology of Hope: On the Ground and Implications of a Christian Eschatology.* Trans. James W. Leitch. New York: Harper and Row, 1967.

———. *The Trinity and the Kingdom: The Doctrine of God.* Trans. Margaret Kohl. New York: Harper and Row, 1981.

———. *The Way of Jesus Christ: Christology in Messianic Dimensions.* Trans. Margaret Kohl. San Francisco: HarperCollins, 1990.

Morell, Virginia. "Evidence Found for a Possible 'Aggression Gene.'" *Science* 260 (18 June 1993): 1722–23.

Moussa, Mario, and Thomas A Shannon. "The Search for the New Pineal Gland: Brain Life and Personhood." *Hastings Center Report* 22 (1992): 30–37.

Murdoch, Iris. *Acastos: Two Platonic Dialogues.* London: Penguin Books, 1986.

Nance, Walter E. "Parables." In *Prescribing Our Future: Ethical Challenges in Genetic Counseling,,* edited by Dianne M. Bartels, Bonnie S. LeRoy, and Arthur L. Caplan. Hawthorne, N.Y.: Aldine de Gruyter, 1993.

National Center for Human Genome Research Office, Office of Communications. "Human Genome Progress" (press release), 16 November 1990.

National Council of Churches. *Genetic Science for Human Benefit.* New York: National Council of the Churches of Christ in the U.S.A., 1986.

National Society of Genetics Counselors. "National Society of Genetic Counselors Code of Ethics." *Journal of Genetic Counseling* 1 (1992): 41–43.

Neuhaus, Richard John, ed. *Guaranteeing the Good Life: Medicine and the Return of Eugenics.* Grand Rapids, Mich.: Wm. B. Eerdmans, 1990.

Niebuhr, H. Richard. *The Responsible Self.* New York: Harper and Row, 1963.

Nolan, Kathleen. "First Fruits: Genetic Screening." *Hastings Center Report* (Special Supplement, July–August, 1992): S2–4.

Nowak, Rachel. "Many Mutations May Make Test Difficult." *Science* 266 (2 December 1994): 1470.

O'Donovan, Oliver. *Begotten or Made?* Oxford, Eng.: Clarendon Press, 1984.

————. *Resurrection and Moral Order: An Outline for Evangelical Ethics.* Grand Rapids, Mich.: Wm. B. Eerdmans, 1986.

Outler, Albert C. "The Beginnings of Personhood: Theological Considerations." *Perkins Journal* 27 (fall 1973): 31.

Pannenberg, Wolfhart. *The Apostles' Creed: In the Light of Today's Questions.* Trans. Margaret Kohl. Philadelphia: Westminster Press, 1972.

————. *Systematic Theology,* vols. 1 and 2. Trans. Geoffrey W. Bromiley. Grand Rapids, Mich.: Wm. B. Eerdmans, 1991, 1994.

Peacocke, Arthur. *Creation and the World of Science.* Oxford, Eng.: Clarendon Press, 1979.

————. *God and the New Biology.* London: Dent, 1986.

————. *Theology for a Scientific Age: Being and Becoming—Natural, Divine and Human.* Minneapolis: Fortress Press, 1993.

Pelikan, Jaroslav. *Christianity and Classical Culture: The Metamorphosis of Natural Theology in the Christian Encounter with Hellenism, The Gifford Lectures, 1992–93.* New Haven, Conn.: Yale University Press, 1993.

Peters, Ted. "Designer Children: The Market World of Reproductive Choice." *Christian Century* 14 (December 1994): 1196.

————. *Sin: Radical Evil in Soul and Society.* Grand Rapids, Mich.: Wm. B. Eerdmans, 1994.

Polkinghorne, John C. *The Faith of a Physicist: Reflections of a Bottom-Up Thinker, The Gifford Lectures for 1993–94.* Princeton, N.J.: Princeton University Press, 1994.

————. *One World.* Princeton, N.J.: Princeton University Press, 1986.

"Principles." In *Genetic Counseling Principles in Action: A Casebook,* edited by Joan H. Marks, Audrey Heimler, Elsa Reich, Nancy S. Wexler, and Susan E. Ince (White Plains, N.Y.: March of Dimes Birth Defects Foundation, 1989).

Ramsey, Paul. *Fabricated Man: The Ethics of Genetic Control.* New Haven, Conn.: Yale University Press, 1970.

————. *The Patient as Person: Explorations in Medical Ethics.* New Haven, Conn.: Yale University Press, 1970.

Rankin, Robert. "Beginnings." In *The Recovery of Spirit in Higher Education: Christian and Jewish Ministries in Campus Life,* edited by Robert Rankin. New York: Seabury Press, 1980.

Robertson, John A. *Children of Choice: Freedom and the New Reproductive Technologies.* Princeton, N.J.: Princeton University Press, 1994.

————. "Procreative Liberty and the Control of Conception, Pregnancy, and Childbirth." *Virginia Law Review* 69 (April 1983): 405–62.

Rothman, Barbara Katz. "Not All That Glitters Is Gold," *Hastings Center Report*, Special Supplement, July–August 1992, S11–15.

———. "The Tentative Pregnancy: Then and Now." In *Women and Prenatal Testing: Facing the Challenges of Genetic Technology*, edited by Karen H. Rothenberg and Elizabeth J. Thomson. Columbus: Ohio State University Press, 1994.

Rucquoi, Jodi K., and M. J. Mahoney. "A Protocol to Address the Depressive Effects of Abortion for Fetal Abnormalities Discovered Prenatally via Amniocentesis." *Psychosocial Aspects of Genetic Counseling*. In March of Dimes Birth Defects Foundation Original Article Series, vol. 28, no. 1, edited by Gerry Evers-Kiebooms, Jean-Pierre Fryns, Jean-Jacques Cassiman, and Herman Van den Berghe. New York: John Wiley, 1992.

Russell, Robert J. "Quantum Physics in Philosophical and Theological Perspective. In *Physics, Philosophy, and Theology: A Common Quest for Understanding*, edited by R. J. Russell, W. R. Stoeger, and C. V. Coyne. Notre Dame, Ind.: University of Notre Dame Press, 1988.

———. "Theistic Evolution: Does God Really Act in Nature?" Typescript paper presented in August 1994, at a consultation on theology and genetics at the Evangelische Akademie Loccum, Germany.

Ryan, Maura A. "The Argument for Unlimited Procreative Liberty: A Feminist Critique." In *Bioethics: Basic Writings on the Key Ethical Questions That Surround the Major, Modern Biological Possibilities and Problems*, 4th ed., edited by Thomas A. Shannon. Mahwah, N.J.: Paulist Press, 1993.

Sass, Hans-Martin. "Brain Life and Brain Death." *Journal of Medicine and Philosophy* 14 (1989): 45–59.

Savitsky, Kinneret, Anat Bar-Shira, Shlomit Gilad, et al. "A Single Ataxia Telangiectasia Gene with a Product Similar to PI-3 Kinase." *Science* 268 (23 June 1995): 1749–53.

Schep, J. A. *The Nature of the Resurrection Body: A Study of the Biblical Data.* Grand Rapids, Mich.: Wm. B. Eerdmans, 1964.

Service, Robert F. "Stalking the Start of Colon Cancer." *Science* 263 (18 March 1994): 1559–60.

Spallone, Patricia. *Beyond Conception: The New Politics of Reproduction.* Granby, Conn.: Bergin and Garvey, 1989.

Suchocki, Marjorie Hewitt. *The End of Evil: Process Eschatology in Historical Context.* Albany: State University of New York Press, 1988.

Thiemann, Ronald F. *Constructing a Public Theology: The Church in a Pluralistic Culture.* Louisville: Westminster John Knox, 1991.

Tibben, A., et al. "Psychological Effects of Presymptomatic DNA Testing for Huntington's Disease in the Dutch Program." *Psychosomatic Medicine* 56 (November–December 1994): 526–32.

United Church of Christ, General Synod 17. "A Pronouncement on the Church and Genetic Engineering." *Social Policy Action.* Cleveland: Office for Church and Society, 1989.

United Methodist Church. "Genetic Science." *The Book of Resolutions of the United Methodist Church 1992.* Nashville, Tenn.: The United Methodist Publishing House, 1992.

Warren, Stephen T., and Claude T. Ashley Jr. "Triplet Repeat Expansion Mutations: The Example of Fragile X Syndrome." *Annual Review of Neuroscience* 18 (1995): 77–99.

Weil, Simone. *Intimations of Christianity among the Ancient Greeks.* Ed. and tran. Elisabeth Chase Geissbuhler. London: Routledge and Kegan Paul, 1957.

Wertz, Dorothy, and John Fletcher. "Attitudes of Genetic Counselors: A Multinational Survey. *American Journal of Human Genetics* 42 (1988): 592–600.

Wood, Linda. "A Glimpse of Grace." *The Cumberland Seminarian* 23, no. 1–2 (fall and spring 1985): 7–10.

World Council of Churches. *Biotechnology: Its Challenges to the Churches and the World.* Geneva: World Council of Churches, Subunit on Church and Society, 1989.

Index

abortion, 40, 81, 93; and genetic testing, xii, 11, 38–40, 108–10, 122, 130, 134–36; "pro-life" movement, 8–9; Roman Catholic Church, 10
Aeschylus, 101
Alzheimer's disease, 26 27, 56
Americans with Disabilities Act, 36
amniocentesis, 16–17; risk from, 17–19, 47, 93
anthropocentrism, 79, 82
Aristotle, 120
Ashley, Claude T., Jr., 144n. 9
ataxia telangiectasia (AT), 27
Augustine of Hippo, 118, 124

baptism, 1–3, 70
Barbour, Ian, 7
Bartholomew, D. J., 151n. 17
Bell Curve, The, 53
Bible and procreation, 8–9, 73–78
Blank, Robert H., 59–60
Bosk, Charles L., 37, 145n. 2
Bouma, Hessel, III, 144n. 9
Breakefield, X. O., 148n. 8
Brunner, H. G., 148n. 8

Calvin, John, 91

cancer, 25–27, 56, 144n. 4
Caplan, Arthur L., 40, 42
Carnley, Peter, 154n. 1
Cases, Olivier, 148n. 8
Cassell, Eric J., 152n. 1
chance, 83–87; and law, 85–87
chorionic villus sampling (CVS), 17, 19
Christology, 118
chromosomes, 20–21, 80
churches, positions on genetics, 9–11
Clarke, Agnus, 136
clergy: male, xiii, 70; role in relation to genetics, xv–xvii, 4, 14, 16, 25, 27–29, 31–32, 34, 43–46, 50, 54, 72, 107
Cobb, John B., Jr., 6
Cole-Turner, Ronald, 148n. 11
Committee on Assessing Genetic Risks, Institute of Medicine, National Academy of Science, 24, 32–33, 42, 45, 59
Corea, Gena, 70
Cowan, Ruth Schwartz, 60–61, 63
creation, doctrine of, 7–8, 48, 64, 74–78, 84–85, 128
Crick, Francis, 20–21